Seven Deadliest Network Attacks

Syngress Seven Deadliest Attacks Series

Seven Deadliest Microsoft Attacks
ISBN: 978-1-59749-551-6
Rob Kraus

Seven Deadliest Network Attacks
ISBN: 978-1-59749-549-3
Stacy Prowell

Seven Deadliest Social Network Attacks
ISBN: 978-1-59749-545-5
Carl Timm

Seven Deadliest Unified Communications Attacks
ISBN: 978-1-59749-547-9
Dan York

Seven Deadliest USB Attacks
ISBN: 978-1-59749-553-0
Brian Anderson

Seven Deadliest Web Application Attacks
ISBN: 978-1-59749-543-1
Mike Shema

Seven Deadliest Wireless Technologies Attacks
ISBN: 978-1-59749-541-7
Brad Haines

Visit **www.syngress.com** for more information on these titles and other resources

Seven Deadliest Network Attacks

Stacy Prowell

Rob Kraus

Mike Borkin

Technical Editor **Chris Grimes**

AMSTERDAM • BOSTON • HEIDELBERG • LONDON
NEW YORK • OXFORD • PARIS • SAN DIEGO
SAN FRANCISCO • SINGAPORE • SYDNEY • TOKYO
Syngress is an imprint of Elsevier

SYNGRESS®

Syngress is an imprint of Elsevier.
30 Corporate Drive, Suite 400, Burlington, MA 01803, USA

This book is printed on acid-free paper.

Notices

Knowledge and best practice in this field are constantly changing. As new research and experience broaden our understanding, changes in research methods, professional practices, or medical treatment may become necessary.

Practitioners and researchers must always rely on their own experience and knowledge in evaluating and using any information, methods, compounds, or experiments described herein. In using such information or methods, they should be mindful of their own safety and the safety of others, including parties for whom they have a professional responsibility.

To the fullest extent of the law, neither the Publisher nor the authors, contributors, or editors assume any liability for any injury and/or damage to persons or property as a matter of products liability, negligence or otherwise, or from any use or operation of any methods, products, instructions, or ideas contained in the material herein.

Library of Congress Cataloging-in-Publication Data
Application submitted

British Library Cataloguing-in-Publication Data
A catalogue record for this book is available from the British Library.

ISBN: 978-1-59749-549-3

Elsevier Inc., the author(s), and any person or firm involved in the writing, editing, or production (collectively "Makers") of this book ("the Work") do not guarantee or warrant the results to be obtained from the Work.

For information on rights, translations, and bulk sales, contact Matt Pedersen, Commercial Sales Director and Rights; e-mail: m.pedersen@elsevier.com

For information on all Syngress publications,
visit our Web site at www.syngress.com

Contents

A preview chapter from *Seven Deadliest Wireless Technologies Attacks* **can be found after the index.**

About the Authors

Stacy Prowell is a senior research scientist in the Cyberspace Sciences and Information Intelligence Research Group at Oak Ridge National Laboratory (ORNL), where he conducts research on cyber security.

Prior to joining ORNL, Stacy worked for the well-known CERT program at Carnegie Mellon University on automated reverse engineering and malware classification. As an industry consultant, Stacy has worked on projects ranging from small, embedded devices to large, distributed, real-time systems and has managed a variety of software development projects. Stacy is a cofounder of Software Silver Bullets, LLC, a company that develops tools to support rigorous software engineering methods.

Stacy holds a PhD from the University of Tennessee and is a senior member of the IEEE and a member of the ACM and Sigma Xi. As this book was being written, Stacy and his family moved to Tennessee, where they now reside. He thanks his family, editors, coauthors, and employers for their amazing patience during this crazy time.

Mike Borkin (CCIE#319568, MCSE) is a director at PigDragon Security, a computer security consulting company, and an internationally known speaker and author. In his professional life, he has worked on developing strategies and securing the infrastructures of many different Fortune 500 companies at both an architectural and engineering level. He has spoken at conferences in both the United States and Europe for various industry groups including SANS, The Open Group, and RSA. This is his third book, having also contributed to *Seven Deadliest Microsoft Attacks* (*Syngress*, ISBN: 978-1-59749-551-6) and coauthored *Windows Vista® Security for Dummies®*.

Mike wishes to thank the coauthors and editors of this book for their dedication and all the hard work that went into bringing it to fruition. He wants to thank his Phi Kappa Tau brothers from the University of Tennessee (Go Vols!) and say that without that brotherhood and the 20+ years of friendship with Stacy Prowell, he would probably be just a janitor. He also wants to thank his family and friends for putting up with him during the process, and especially Melissa (‖) for what she has to deal with on an everyday basis. He especially hopes that the information in this book provides you with a better understanding of how to secure network environments while still taking the time to entertain.

Rob Kraus (CISSP, CEH, MCSE) is a Senior Security Consultant for Solutionary, Inc. Rob is responsible for organizing customer requirements, on-site project management, and client support while ensuring quality and timeliness of Solutionary's products and services.

Rob was previously a Remote Security Services Supervisor with Digital Defense, Inc. He performed offensive-based security assessments consisting of penetration testing, vulnerability assessment, social engineering, wireless and VoIP penetration testing, web application penetration tests, and vulnerability research. As a supervisor,

Rob was also responsible for leading and managing a team of penetration testers who performed assessment services for Digital Defense's customers.

Rob's background also includes contracting as a security analyst for AT&T during the early stages of the AT&T U-verse service, as well as provisioning, optimizing, and testing OC-192 fiber-optic networks while employed with Nortel Networks.

Rob also speaks at information security conferences and universities in an effort to keep the information security community informed of current security trends and attack methodologies.

Rob is currently attending the University of Phoenix, completing his Bachelor of Science in Information Technology/Software Engineering, and he resides in San Antonio, TX, with his wife Kari, son Soren, and daughter Kylee.

Technical Editor

Chris Grimes (CISSP#107943, GSEC, GCIA, CEH) is a Senior Security Consultant with Roche Pharmaceuticals. He provides information security solutions in the areas of vulnerability management, intrusion detection, forensics and e-Discovery, Web application security, antivirus, and database security. Chris has worked for Eli Lilly, as well as IQuest Internet.

Introduction

BOOK OVERVIEW AND KEY LEARNING POINTS

Security is heavily *contextual*; the effectiveness of any security measures depends on the context into which they are deployed. What if you give keys to the janitor, and he or she leaves them in his or her unlocked car? Further security is often *not incremental*; insecurity in one area can lead to insecurity in *all* areas. Hackers might break into your machines and steal your proposals and bidding information, so you carefully secure your network. Hackers might break into employees' home networks to steal passwords, e-mail accounts, or even hijack "secure" connections to break into your corporate network, so you institute policies about remote access. Hackers might park outside your building and "listen in" on your wireless network, so you encrypt it and use special measures to prevent the wireless signal from leaking outside the building. Hackers might use e-mail "phishing" and other "social engineering" attacks to gain access, so you add more policies and carefully train your staff and test them from time to time. Finally, comfortably secure and ready for anything, you unknowingly hire the hackers and fall victim to an "insider" attack. Life's tough.

What we think of as security is really a collection of policies and procedures that are, ultimately, about *giving out* information. Your employees (or even other parts of your infrastructure) *need* information to accomplish their mission. Security stands between your employees and accomplishing that mission. All too often serious security breaches start with some otherwise well-intentioned effort to get some useful work done. Sometimes, it is your employees who break your security; not necessarily because they have some evil purpose, but sometimes because they believe the mission is more important or that the security measures are unnecessary. The mission may be short term and absolutely critical. The effects of a security breach can take years to evolve or even to be detected.

It is late in the day and you have a very important bet-your-company deliverable due out in the morning. You desperately need Software X to run in order to finish the deliverable, but Software X is being blocked by your firewall. You've tried adding rules to the firewall, you've tried calling the vendor, but nothing is working. Finally you disable the firewall, finish the deliverable, and ship. Will you remember to re-enable the firewall? Did you monitor your network while the firewall was down? The view that security is a collection of tradeoffs, or a series of calculated risks, assumes a *continuous* nature to security. The belief that you can trade *a little* insecurity for some other gain is often a misunderstanding of the nature of security. This is akin to saying you will allow anyone to withdraw money from your bank account but only as much as they can withdraw in 10 minutes. The mistake is that the two things (in this case money and time) are not directly related.

HOW THIS BOOK IS ORGANIZED

This book identifies seven classes of network attacks and discusses how the attack works, including tools to accomplish the attack, what are the risks of the attack, and how to defend against the attack. Seven attacks were chosen: denial of service, war dialing, penetration testing, protocol tunneling, spanning tree attacks, man-in-the-middle, and password replay. These are not mutually exclusive; you can exploit the spanning tree protocol, for example, to launch a denial-of-service attack. These were chosen because they help illustrate different aspects of network security; the principles on which they rely are unlikely to vanish any time soon, and they allow for the possibility of gaining something of interest to the attacker, from money to high-value data.

Chapter 1, "Denial of Service," illustrates how even sophisticated networks can be crippled by a determined hacker with relatively few resources.

Chapter 2, "War Dialing," illustrates how a hacker can circumvent the hardened security perimeter of a network to access "softer" targets.

Chapter 3, "Penetration 'Testing,'" discusses the various tools and techniques used for penetration testing that are readily available to both the defenders *and* the attackers.

Chapter 4, "Protocol Tunneling," presents a method for deliberately subverting your network perimeter to "tunnel" prohibited traffic into and out of your network.

Chapter 5, "Spanning Tree Attacks," discusses the "layer 2" network responsible for knitting together your switches, routers, and other devices into a reliable network, and illustrates one way in which to exploit the weak security of this layer.

Chapter 6, "Man-in-the-Middle," discusses a very common attack pattern and just what an attacker can accomplish once he or she has inserted himself or herself into your data stream.

Chapter 7, "Password Replay," focuses on the security of passwords and other static security measures and how an attacker can use various techniques to gain unauthorized access.

This book is intended to provide practical, usable information. However, the world of network security is evolving very rapidly, and the attack that works today may (hopefully) not work tomorrow. It is more important, then, to understand the principles on which the attacks and exploits are based in order to properly plan either a network attack or a network defense. The authors chose the contents of this book because we believe that, underlying the attacks presented here, there are important principles of network security. The attacks are deadly because they exploit principles, assumptions, and practices that are true today and that we believe are likely to remain true for the foreseeable future.

Increasingly sophisticated criminal organizations launch network attacks as a serious, for-profit enterprise. Similarly, well-funded governmental actors launch network attacks for political reasons or for intelligence gathering. Cyberspace is already a battlefield. Even if your network doesn't have high-value intelligence and you don't have deep pockets, you may be the target of a sophisticated attack because you have something else of value: machines and network access. An attacker may exploit your network to launch malware or to launch a network attack. Your Internet Protocol address may serve to give the attacker a level of plausible deniability. After all, would you want to launch the virus you just finished creating through your own Internet service provider connection? Attackers may use your machines for storage of information ranging from child pornography to stolen credit card numbers. Once these show up on your machines, it becomes your job to explain how they got there. Attackers can use compromised machines for command and control of deployed and distributed malware. This can result in your network being blacklisted or blocked as a distribution source for malware. Is this the company image you want your customers to see?

As networks grow and incorporate more sophisticated technologies, it can become difficult to maintain the necessary situational awareness. What were once "dumb" network nodes such as printers and network hardware may now have exploitable – and unexpected – vulnerabilities. These components are – in reality – just other computers on the network. Some of them have multiple interfaces that need to be considered, including Bluetooth, wireless, and wired connections. If one interface is well protected and another disabled, there may still be a third that is available. Network security requires considering the role and security concerns of each device, not just delivering the device and plugging it in.

There are many reasons why network security is hard, ranging from the fact that networks are increasingly sophisticated and complex to the fact that economic incentives can work against proper security. Network security is essentially *asymmetric warfare*; your adversaries can probe anywhere, but you have to defend everywhere. This creates a technological bias in favor of the attackers. Further, criminal organizations live in a target-rich environment. If they are unsuccessful with one attack, they can move on and attack a different organization.

The market for computer security products can – and does – fall prey to the *asymmetric information* problem. This is a case in which buyers of a product do not have as much information about the relative merits of the product as the sellers do. This creates a downward pressure on prices that, in turn, creates a downward pressure on quality.

Consider a used car market in which there are 100 good cars (the "plums"), worth $3000 each, and 100 rather troublesome ones (the "lemons"), each of which is worth only $1000. The vendors know which is which, but the buyers don't. So what will be the equilibrium price of used cars?

If customers start off believing that the probability that they will get a plum is equal to the probability that they will get a lemon, then the market price will start off at $2000. However, at that price only lemons will be offered for sale, and once the buyers observe this, the price will drop rapidly to $1000 with no plums being sold at all.[1]

CONCLUSION

Network security depends on many factors, and perfect network security is impossible. Network protocols can be inherently insecure in surprising ways. Cryptographic functions that are essential to network security can fall prey to sophisticated mathematical attacks. The algorithms that implement protocols or cryptography can contain bugs. Even otherwise correct code can fall prey to the effects of being run on a computer; errors exist in chip designs, and the use of finite-precision math on computers can result in unexpected effects that can be exploited. This is all good news for attackers—but not so much for defenders.

Of course, all is not lost. As a network administrator, you may have other factors on your side, including support by law enforcement, governmental agencies, and trusted third parties such as CERT[A] and SANS.[B] You have to control what you can. Stay educated on threats and responses. Make sure procedures support good security, and that personnel are properly trained. Make plans to deal with attacks. Most importantly, you need to understand how and why network attacks work. It is our hope that this book will contribute to that goal.

Endnote

1. Anderson R. Why information security is hard – an economic perspective. Proceedings of the 17th Annual Computer Security Applications Conference (ACSAC); 2001 Dec.

[A] See www.cert.org/
[B] See www.sans.org/

Denial of Service

1

INFORMATION IN THIS CHAPTER

- How Denial of Service Works
- Dangers of Denial of Service
- Defense against Denial of Service
- The Future of Denial of Service

On April 26, 2007, the nation of Estonia was hit with a denial-of-service (DoS) attack. The attack lasted, off and on, until May 18th of the same year. The attack effectively cut off Internet access for much of the country. Members of the Parliament could not access their e-mail, people were unable to access their online banking accounts, Estonian news agencies could not communicate outside the country's borders, ATMs ceased to work, and citizens traveling abroad discovered their debit cards no longer worked.[1]

Estonia was not overcome because of outdated infrastructure. It was (and is) one of the most "wired" countries in Europe, thanks to their Tiigrihüpe (Tiger's Leap) project. In Estonia, as in France and Greece, Internet access is regarded as a basic human right, and the Estonian government has invested heavily in information technology (IT).

One might also be tempted to dismiss an Internet outage as nothing serious. Of course, if your business depends on the Internet, you may feel differently. Estonia's largest bank, Hansabank, is estimated to have lost around $1 million as the result of the attack. Banks are increasingly dependent on Internet banking and foreign money transfers, and thus an "always on" Internet. If the Internet *is* your business, as with Amazon.com and eBay, the effect can be disastrous.

Was this attack the result of careful planning by a foreign government? It now seems likely that the attack was organized and coordinated by one man: a 22-year-old Russian named Konstantin Goloskokov. He apparently carried out the attack in protest of the Estonian government's decision to move the Bronze Soldier, a war monument in Tallinn erected by the Soviet Union in 1947. At the time of writing, the Estonian government has arrested and convicted just one person: Dmitri Galushkevich, who took part in the attack working from his laptop.

DoS attacks are on the rise and can be perpetrated by large-state actors, experienced hackers, or even by novices ("script kiddies") following any of the "how-to" manuals found on the Internet. DoS attacks can be launched for any number of reasons, from political protest to espionage and even extortion. These attacks can be intentional, like the one just described, or unintentional, like the "Slashdot" effect.

As an example of unintentional DoS, suppose several aggregators, including Slashdot[A] and Digg,[B] pick up your essay on why Data was the best acting captain in *Star Trek* history. Now, thousands of people are visiting your site every minute, and the bandwidth allocated to you by your Internet service provider (ISP) is quickly used up. Now *nobody* can get to your site, not even you. Worst of all, you can't post the adorable video of your cats dressed as the crew of the enterprise. You've been the victim of unintentional DoS. You may even get a bill from your ISP for the extra bandwidth.

This chapter will focus on intentional DoS – a denial-of-service *attack*. DoS attacks can be launched for a number of reasons; the Estonia case was a sort of protest but they can be used to damage competitors for financial gain. In 2004, businessman Saad "Jay" Echouafni allegedly hired computer hackers to launch a DoS attack on three of his competitors. Another application of DoS attacks for financial gain is extortion. A company receives a threat that they will be subjected to a DoS attack unless they wire money to an offshore account. In many cases, the company will simply pay. In 2004, Carnegie Mellon University surveyed 100 companies. They found that 17% of medium-size businesses had been the target of some form of cyber-extortion.[C]

HOW DENIAL OF SERVICE WORKS

DoS requires two elements: a resource of finite capacity, and the means to acquire or "use up" the resource faster than it can be replenished. Although we generally think of these attacks in terms of computers, DoS attacks do not have to be network-based. It is possible to have "real-world" DoS attacks, provided you have the above two elements.

Real-world examples include the practice of "land blocking" where a company purchases the land around a store to prevent competitors from opening nearby, and many of the methods used by DeBeers to control the diamond market in the twentieth century.[D] These are examples of a single entity that is powerful enough to consume

---

[A]http://slashdot.org/
[B]http://digg.com/
[C]As of August 2009, the full report is available online: http://heinz-racer.heinz.cmu.edu/whatsnew/images/CMU_Cyber_Extortion_Study.pdf.
[D]For an excellent history of the diamond market, see *The Diamond Ring: Business, Politics, and Precious Stones in South Africa, 1867–1947*, by Colin Newbury, Oxford University Press, 1990.

enough of the available resources (land, diamond production, or any resource your competition needs) to disrupt or starve others. In general, this requires deep pockets or significant resources, which makes it much less likely to occur than DoS attacks in the virtual world.

Distributed Denial of Service

To conduct a successful DoS attack, you usually need a lot of help. This is the origin of the *distributed* denial of service attack (DDoS). As an example of a DDoS attack for the physical world, consider the following: you admire the cool-headed reasoned approach of Captain Picard over the random cowboy style of Captain Kirk, and decide that what the world needs is a statue of Picard in San Francisco, the (future) home of Starfleet. To this end, you start a campaign to raise money, and people begin sending you checks.

Sadly your "friend" Mike does not agree and makes his mission to stop you. He recruits friends to send you hate mail, and soon your mailbox is stuffed with angry letters about why Kirk is better than Picard. Sorting through the mail takes longer and longer, and you only find a few checks in every batch of letters. Soon you've got friends involved to sort the mail, but sending the same angry letter multiple times is easier (and cheaper) than sending a new check, so the volume of hate mail far outstrips the volume of checks. You need more and more time to sort the mail, for fewer payoffs.

Everyday your mailbox is stuffed full. The post office begins to hold your mail because it cannot deliver it. Now you must drive to the post office to collect boxes of (mostly) photocopied hate mail, and you have to open every letter because you can't easily tell which ones contain checks. Ultimately you may have to abandon your quest, noble though it may be.

Although a DDoS attack is hard to pull off in the physical world, DDoS is the most common – and disturbing – form of DoS attack in the virtual one. Utilizing DDoS techniques and the Internet, small groups (or even a single individual) can conduct massive DoS attacks. The rest of this chapter will focus solely on DDoS attacks.

Overview of a Denial of Service Attack

Suppose you want to conduct a network DDoS attack against a particular *victim*. You are taking the role commonly called the *intruder*. To conduct a DDoS attack, you need to be able to "use up" some resource needed by the victim. You can target any resource likely to interrupt your target. For instance, if you are targeting an online retailer, you might do any of the following.

- Overload the Web servers.
- Overload any network link.
- Crash servers.
- Attack a dependency.

In the last case you don't attack the victim directly, but you might attack their bank, their credit card clearing company, their accounting firm, or one of their suppliers, making it impossible for them to conduct business.

It is likely that your target, especially if it is a bank or online retailer, has a lot of capacity you must use up before you are successful. Your computer just cannot generate enough network traffic to launch a successful DDoS attack. You need help.

In some cases, it may be possible to use social engineering to accomplish your goal. For example, if you can start a successful Internet rumor about your victim, you may be able to get others to do your work for you. For example, you might post a long and official-looking "news" story about how your "friend" Mike was caught raising Dalmatian puppies for their fur. Soon activists are calling him at all hours, filling *his* mailbox with hate mail, and even stopping by his house. Mike can no longer go to the store, let alone continue his DDoS attack against you. Sadly, his friends may carry on in his absence.

Most often you will instead attempt to gain control of a large number of computers from which to conduct the attack. During the 1990s, you might have targeted universities because they had large numbers of always-connected machines with fast connections and (typically) low security. Today, university networks are better protected and monitored, but the rapid growth of the Internet means you can find a large number of always-connected machines with reasonably fast connections and low security in peoples' homes and small businesses. If you can compromise enough of these machines, you can launch your attack.

EPIC FAIL

If you aren't careful, you can launch a DDoS attack on yourself. In 2003, the University of Wisconsin at Madison was flooded by as many as 280,000 Network Time Protocol (NTP) packets per second. The source? Netgear routers (about 700,000 of them) were sending requests for the current time. These routers were configured such that, if no answer was returned within 1 s, they sent another request. If a router got a satisfactory reply, it would then wait for a period of time and update again. Once the system at Madison became congested, this approach (try again every second) just made matters worse, and even machines with a satisfactory reply would be asking again before the queue had been cleared.[2]

At the time of the writing of this book, the largest networks of compromised machines are believed to be the Conficker and Srizbi *botnets*, containing around 1 million and 450,000 compromised computers, respectively. Its primary use is sending spam; a different sort of DDoS attack that slows your ability to read your e-mail.

Recruitment

This initial phase of collecting machines you can control, or *zombies*, is called *recruitment*. During the recruitment phase, you need to find machines you can take over. The process of looking for vulnerable machines is called *scanning*. While scanning can be done manually, it is obviously better to let computers do the work.

Several network scanners exist to find vulnerable machines, including Nmap,[E] Nessus,[F] and SAINT.[G] You can specify particular machines to scan, scan entire blocks of the network, or scan randomly for vulnerable machines. These tools can help you discover vulnerable machines on your network so you can patch or remove them. Alternately, they can be used to find vulnerable machines on *other people's* networks so that you can make them into zombies.

Figure 1.1 shows the result of a network scan using Nmap. The Zenmap graphical user interface is shown. Figure 1.2 shows a vulnerability detected using Nessus.

Exploitation

Once you've found machines that are vulnerable, you can move on to *exploit*, or gain access to, the machines. There are many ways to exploit a machine, depending on what operating system and patches are installed. Once again, this is a task best turned

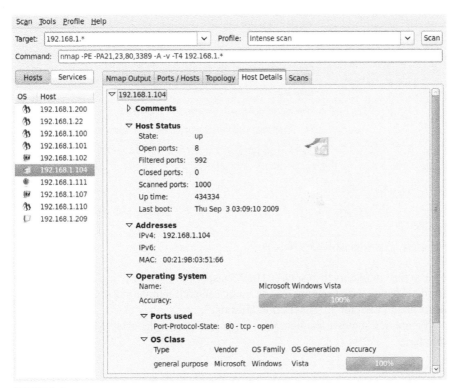

FIGURE 1.1

Scanning a Network with Nmap

[E]http://nmap.org/

[F]Nessus is a registered trademark of Tenable Network Security: www.nessus.org/nessus/. An open-source version of this tool called OpenVAS also exists: http://openvas.org/.

[G]SAINT is a registered trademark of SAINT Corporation: www.saintcorporation.com/.

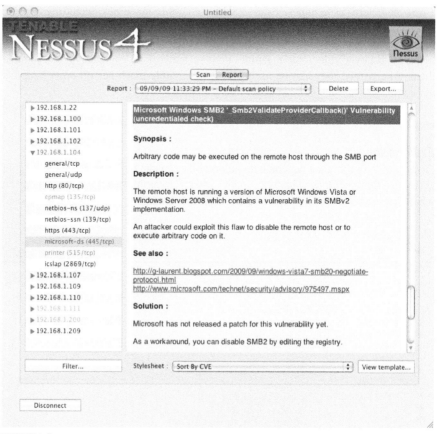

FIGURE 1.2

Detecting a Vulnerability Using Nessus

over to the computers themselves. The Metasploit Framework[H] is a tool specifically for developing and executing exploit code against a remote machine, and its use is described in Chapter 3, "Penetration 'Testing'".

Figure 1.3 shows a configuration page for an exploit, using Metasploit's Web interface.

Installation

Now that you have found and exploited a vulnerable machine, you need to install the *payload* software. This software typically includes several items.

- Task-oriented software to perform the actual DDoS attack.
- Command-and-control software so you can control, coordinate, and launch the attack.

[H]www.metasploit.com/

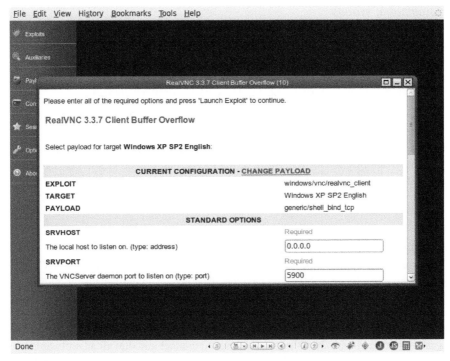

FIGURE 1.3

Configuring an Exploit with Metasploit

- Antidetection software to prevent your software from being discovered and removed.
- Update software so you can remotely update the machine.

Control

The software to control the machine is typically called a *bot* (short for "robot"), and the resulting network of machines is called a *botnet*. The bot listens for specific control strings on an Internet Relay Chat (IRC) channel and responds on the channel or takes other actions. It is not uncommon for compromised machines to act as IRC "routers" (to pass along messages) and "proxies" (to hide the fact that IRC is being used).

More recently, some botnets have been found that use instant messaging (IM) and even Twitter[1] for command and control. Any lightweight, decentralized network will do. IM can even be used for the infection phase, by sending a malicious link for a user to click, or by exploiting a vulnerability in an IM client.

---

[1]http://twitter.com/

Automation: Worms

You can proceed to compromise more machines, but one approach is to take the above process and embed it in a worm. A *worm* is a program that *automatically* propagates from one vulnerable machine to another. The worm automates the scan-exploit-install process, copying itself to each exploited machine, and then using that machine to launch further attacks. This gives several advantages:

- The scanning and exploitation of machines is parallelized, so you can grow your botnet much faster.
- You may find helpful information on the machine itself, such as the addresses of other machines in a local network or log files containing other addresses you can scan.
- The path used to exploit a machine is very difficult to trace back, making it harder to find you.

Propagation

The worm may or may not contain the payload. Some worms "phone home" after exploiting a machine to obtain the payload. This is convenient because it allows the intruder to manage the payload centrally. This is convenient for the defender (your intended victim) because they can potentially detect or defeat you by watching for or by blocking communication with your host. The SoBig worm used this method; it was programmed with 20 different addresses to contact and download software.[J]

Other worms may use a "back-chaining" method, where a worm propagating from host A to host B first exploits host B, and then later pulls the payload from host A. This can be useful if the payload is large, and the transfer may be interrupted, perhaps by a network outage. The worm can resume the transfer later when the network is again available. This also gives the worm a chance to disable scanning and antivirus programs before installing the payload, perhaps reducing the chances of detection. The Ramen worm that infected Linux machines used this method. Finally, the worm may act as a single program, containing both the propagation software and the payload. The tiny, but virulent SQL Slammer worm used this method, as did the Morris worm.

NOTE

Many regard the Morris worm as the first computer worm. A mistake in the worm's propagation code resulted in a severe, though unintended, DoS attack. This led DARPA (the United States Department of Defense Advanced Research Projects Agency) to fund the creation of the CERT/CC at Carnegie Mellon University to serve as a central point for coordinating responses to network emergencies. The cost of removing the Morris worm has been estimated at between $10 million and $100 million.

[J]SoBig illustrates some difficulties in classifying malware. It can propagate on its own, so it is a worm, but it can also "pretend" to be an innocuous e-mail attachment, so it may be classified as a Trojan horse.

Different variants of the Conficker worm use different propagation methods. Interestingly, some variants select domain names based on the date, and then try to contact each of them. This creates many potential rendezvous points for the intruder to control and update the worm, while making it hard to defeat the worm by blacklisting or detecting addresses.[K]

The worm may find new machines to infect by randomly trying addresses, but it is also possible to provide the worm with a "hit list" of address blocks to try, so that the propagation is not completely random. For instance, you may want to avoid scanning certain targets (such as network security sites), since the worm may be detected. You might also want to avoid certain hosts for legal reasons. Some malware avoids infecting machines in certain countries, possibly so the author can avoid prosecution by the local authorities. Swizzor will not infect machines using the Russian language version of Windows, and Conficker does not infect machines using a Ukrainian keyboard layout.

Launching the Attack

Now that you have a botnet, you are ready to launch the attack. At this point, there are several methods open to you:

- You can preschedule your attack, embedding it in the worm itself. In this case, you do not need to communicate with the infected machines, possibly reducing the chances you will be discovered. On the other hand, this approach is far less flexible.
- You can send a command to your botnet to initiate an attack, perhaps of a specific duration and type. This allows you to collect information about the result of the attack, and then plan the next phase.

The only remaining item is what you specifically do to the victim. Again, you have several options:

- **Crash machines** By exploiting vulnerability in operating system software, you may be able to cause a machine to fail or reboot. The *teardrop* attack is an example of this kind of attack.[L]
- **"Break" something** It may even be possible in some instances to corrupt the machine's code so that it will not successfully reboot. This is sometimes called *permanent* DoS or "phlashing." If you can corrupt the firmware (the most basic programming a machine uses to start itself) or the boot sector of a hard disk (the code used to load the operating system when the machine boots up), you may be able to "brick" the machine, or permanently disable it.
- **Overwhelm something** This is the classic distributed DoS and is discussed in more detail below.

[K]For a lot of analysis of Conficker, visit the Conficker Working Group on the Web, at www.confickerworkinggroup.org/.

[L]Long messages sent on the Internet must be broken into a sequence of packets. These packets are then sent, and reassembled into the original message at the destination. The *teardrop* attack exploits this by creating and sending a series of bogus packets that overlap, are too large, or otherwise do not constitute a valid message when reassembled. This exploits bugs in the reassembly algorithm; when the receiver tries to assemble the packets into a complete message, it crashes.

As with scanning and exploitation, there are ready-made toolkits to get you started. Agobot is an open-source worm that requires very little programming skill to use. It has been released under an open-source license, has since been specialized with many variants, and includes a variety of features for propagation and for conducting DDoS attacks.[M] There are many other well-known DDoS tools, including Trinoo, Shaft, and Stacheldraht.[N]

Ping Floods

There are many ways to overwhelm your victim. Most of these rely on exploiting Internet protocols, but it is often possible to overwhelm a host by simply sending lots of otherwise legitimate messages.

Suppose you are headed to a *Star Trek* convention where you will have the chance to actually meet Patrick Stewart. Sadly, if anyone says hello to you and offers to shake your hand, you are obligated to say "hello" back and shake their hand. Upon arriving you are greeted by your "friend" Mike and 300 or so people he rounded up for this event. You spend the entire time saying hello and shaking hands, and never get to see Patrick Stewart. You've just been the victim of a *ping flood*.

Internet Control Message Protocol (ICMP) is one of the foundational protocols on which the Internet is built. To determine whether a particular host is accessible and working or to determine the *latency*, or time to communicate with a host, ICMP provides a special kind of message called an *echo request*, or more commonly, *ping*.[O] Ping messages are used to measure the round-trip time for a message to reach a destination and return, as well as to gauge the quality of a connection.

When a machine receives an ICMP echo request (ping), it must reply to the sender with an ICMP echo reply containing the same data as the original request. In other words, if someone says hello you must say hello back. Because of this requirement, if you flood the victim with pings from many different hosts you can overwhelm the machine, and it will spend all its time and network bandwidth replying to pings, creating a very effective DDoS attack. This has become less useful in recent years, as many network administrators have started filtering ping messages at the edge of their network, or simply by shutting off the ICMP echo server.

There are many variants on this theme, including SYN floods (another kind of Internet message that can use up resources), and the "Smurf" attack that combines pings with a special network address called the *broadcast address* to use up network bandwidth.

[M]Agobot is an example of a "kit." It provides an extensible shell for implementing new exploits. Included with Agobot is a set of helpful notes explaining how to build Agobot, and some later versions (Phatbot) include a GUI to assist in customization.

[N]The source for these and other malware can be found on the Packet Storm Web site: http://packetstormsecurity.org/

[O]The technical details of the Internet are found in a series of documents called requests for comments, or RFCs, and you can find them at many sites, including www.faqs.org/. The ICMP echo request and reply messages are detailed in RFC 792 and RFC 1122.

DNS Amplification Attacks

Another part of the Internet's infrastructure can be exploited for a DDoS attack. Domain name service (DNS) is responsible for translating a host name like google.com into a network address that can be used to actually connect to the host. A request for a network address can be very small (a few bytes), but yield a very large reply (a few kilobytes). This effect is called *amplification* and is the key to this kind of attack.

Machines in your botnet send out special messages to domain name servers requesting a lookup of an address. The messages sent are *spoofed*. That is, they lie about their return address so that they appear to come from your victim. The replies generated by the servers then flood the victim, choking off its network bandwidth, and making it unavailable. It is quite common to use spoofing to hide the source of an attack.

This attack depends on finding name servers (called *open resolvers*) that will answer a recursive query for any host. Name servers are not required to answer recursive queries, but sometimes are incorrectly configured to do so. In a *nonrecursive* query (also called an *iterative* query), a client asks a name server about a hostname. If the name server does not directly know the hostname, it replies with a referral to another, more authoritative name server. The client should then query that server. This process may repeat several times, resulting ultimately in either failure or success. A name server configured to perform a *recursive* query does all this work on behalf of the client.

Service-Level DDoS

You may also attack your victim by sending a flood of legitimate-looking service requests. For instance, you might have all the machines in your botnet flood a Web server with requests for pages. This is a *service-level* DDoS attack, and it is very hard to detect and defend.

A Web server can typically handle a certain volume of traffic for a page. Suppose that a Web server can handle at most 5,000 requests per second for a particular page. Given this, a botnet of 10,000 machines can easily generate 5,000 requests per second, leaving the Web server maxed out. Additional, legitimate traffic only gets through occasionally, resulting in timeout failures. In this case, the DDoS attack may not be evident to the victim at all, though legitimate users of the Web service are affected.

Further, the Web server can successfully respond to all requests, but still fail from the point of legitimate requests. During a DDoS attack, your server may have to handle 1,000 bogus requests generated as part of the attack for every legitimate request. If each request must be handled in turn, then the 1,000 bogus requests will delay servicing of the legitimate request. Even if it is eventually handled, the user may have observed a significant delay, given up, and moved on. They may try their request again later, or they may simply move on to one of your competitors, remembering that your site is slow.

It is also possible to exploit the computational cost of certain operations to affect a DDoS attack with much less traffic. Requesting a simple HTML page from a server is quite different from searching a product catalog or trying to log in. If you can find an operation on a site that requires significant computation, you can target that operation in your attack. One emerging tactic is to flood a site with bogus login requests, as checking a user name and password takes longer to handle than a simple page request. This approach relies on computational properties of the requests and can be though of as a *semantic* DDoS attack.

DANGERS OF DENIAL OF SERVICE

If your DDoS attack exploits a vulnerability of your victim, you may only need to generate a very small amount of traffic. If you can successfully crash a machine, you may cause your victim to suffer downtime, lose business, or even lose customer data. This gives DDoS a high payoff for a low input.

Flood attacks require generating a lot more traffic, but require significantly less sophistication to conduct. If you can generate enough legitimate-looking Web traffic, you can flood a Web server and shut down an online business. Again, there is a high payoff for a (relatively) low effort.

The use of botnets helps insulate intruder from the victim, making it harder to track down and prosecute the intruder. Further, if you can grow a large botnet, you can extort money from many large companies, and even conduct more than one DDoS attack at a time. Some people accumulate botnets and then essentially lease them to others to conduct the actual DDoS attack.

A DDoS attack is especially deadly because of key factors:

- It is *simple*. Recruit many machines and have them flood your target with legitimate-looking traffic. There are many automated tools to download, along with tutorials and other help for inexperienced users. Even tools that have been around for years are still very effective and can be used with little or even no modification and tweaking.
- It is *effective*. With enough machines generating traffic you can bring down even the largest targets, either by overloading their servers, or by consuming all the network bandwidth.
- It is *cheap*. DDoS attacks use other people's resources, in the form of zombie machines. The tools and information necessary to conduct a DDoS attack are available for free on the Internet. All that an intruder really requires is access to a computer to launch the attack.
- It can be fairly *safe*. If your victim is in a different country it may be very hard, or even impossible, to arrest you, even if your identity is discovered. Konstantin Goloskokov, the self-identified leader of the Estonia attack described at the start of this chapter, remains at large and it is unlikely he will be prosecuted. To be sure, this last point depends on where you live, and whom you choose as your victim. As mentioned previously, intruders often intentionally avoid exploiting machines in their home country.

As more economic activity moves onto the Internet, the use of DDoS for extortion, terrorism, and other purposes will increase. In particular, DDoS extortion leverages a high payoff from a low cost of entry. While people have been caught and prosecuted for such cyber crime, it is widely assumed that, at least at present, many companies prefer to simply pay a "reasonable" amount to avoid disruption, and do not report the incident to law enforcement. Extortion has become a cost of doing business on the Internet.

DEFENSE AGAINST DENIAL OF SERVICE

Recall the two essential ingredients of a DoS attack.

- A resource of finite capacity, and
- The means to acquire or "use up" the resource faster than it can be replenished.

This immediately suggests one possible defense strategy: increase the capacity of the resource, or the rate at which the resource is replenished. Returning to the earlier example of the Picard/Kirk letter campaign, increasing the capacity of the resource is like getting a bigger mailbox; increasing the rate at which the resource is replenished is like getting more friends to help you sort your mail. As you can probably tell, neither approach guarantees success. It is still easier for your enemies to generate work for you than it is for you to do that work.

You can make a list of the people who send you hate mail, and discard letters from those people. That is, you *blacklist* certain senders. Unfortunately, the senders don't include return addresses on the envelopes, or sometimes *spoof* their return address, giving someone else's instead. This tricks you into opening the letter from Aunt Martha to discover another rant about how Kirk was the only real captain of the Enterprise. You can also base your blacklist on the postmark, and begin dropping all mail from certain zip codes. This means you are going to discard some checks, too (*false positives*). This strategy corresponds to blocking Internet Protocol (IP) address ranges.

The only completely effective way to secure against a DDoS attack is to secure a very large portion of the machines attached to the Internet against misuse. Unfortunately, this is impractical because the Internet spans political and even continental boundaries. Keeping machines up-to-date on patches can help prevent them from becoming part of a botnet. Sadly, when a security hole is detected, an exploit can often be generated long before a patch is available. When a patch is released it is typically hours, and sometimes days, before machines are updated. The *automated* generation of exploit code from the patch has been demonstrated, and typically takes only minutes.[P]

The lesson here is that completely securing machines against a DDoS attack is probably not possible (though we should certainly try!). Much of the focus must be on *survivability* instead of security. That is, it may be impossible to prevent a DDoS attack, but you can take steps to survive the attack.

[P]See David Brumley, *et al.*, "Automatic Patch-Based Exploit Generation is Possible: Techniques and Implications," in the *Proceedings of the IEEE Security and Privacy Symposium*, May 2008.

General Advice

Before we get into the details of defending yourself against a DDoS attack, here are a few pieces of general advice:

- If you are the victim of a DDoS attack, save your traffic logs, record everything you observe, and keep a record of everything you do. This is essential if you intend to work with law enforcement to try to track down the intruder, but also provides a record you can use after the attack to better understand what happened and how you can better defend your network in the future.
- Keep yourself up to date on DDoS attack methods and defenses. New articles are routinely published and contain trends and other information to help you better plan and update your network defenses.
- Monitor your network for vulnerable systems. Running tools like Nessus and Nmap (see the "Recruitment" section) can help you quickly identify vulnerable systems on your network.
- Routinely scan your machines to make sure that they are not part of a botnet. It will not look good if an attack against one of your competitors is traced back to your machines.
- Enable logging and monitor log files for suspicious activity. There are tools to help you do this, called *intrusion detection systems* (IDS). These tools can also help you detect an attack and will be discussed in more detail in the section "IDS/IPS Systems."
- Establish a routine for updating, scanning, and monitoring so that these activities are carried out routinely and regularly. Organizations such as CERT[Q] and SANS[R] publish guidelines on best practices. Make yourself familiar with these.

TIP

The "InfoSec" reading room on the SANS Institute site contains white papers on a variety of topics, including incident handling. See www.sans.org/. The CERT Web site has a section for system administrators that includes vulnerability information and freely available tools including AirCERT, which provides for automated incident reporting. See www.cert.org/.

WARNING

While it is a good idea to run a tool like Nessus on your own network, you should be careful when configuring a scan to avoid accidentally scanning outside your network. In some cases, your ISP may detect the scan and simply shut down your access. In other cases, like scanning your employer's network, you may receive an unwanted visit from the IT department. Running scanners is typically against network policy; use them on your own network, only.

[Q]www.cert.org/
[R]www.sans.org/

Strategy

The general life cycle of an incident response is to *protect* against attacks, *detect* attacks, and finally *react* to attacks.[S] Each of these stages is essential to an overall strategy for dealing with DDoS attacks. The remaining sections of this chapter provide details about how to defend against DDoS attacks. Keep in mind that this is a rapidly changing environment, and that what works today may not work tomorrow. It is essential that you keep yourself up to date on DDoS defense.

Network Configuration

Understand your network and make sure that it is configured correctly. This is fundamental both to preventing DDoS attacks and to preventing your machines from being used to launch a DDoS attack. First, and perhaps simplest, block any unused ports at the network edge. In particular, ports 6665 through 6669 (tcp) have traditionally been used for IRC, though of course any port may be used.

One way to prevent your machines from being used in a DDoS attack (or at least to make it less likely to succeed) is to guard against address spoofing. Recall that every message has an embedded return address. It is typical to alter, or *spoof* this address when conducting a DDoS attack to make it harder to properly block incoming traffic, or to even determine the origin of the traffic at all.

Configure routers and firewalls at the edge of your network to filter *outgoing* packets from your network whose address field does not match your network's address. That is, if an outgoing packet has an address that is not from your network, discard the packet.

Some DDoS attacks use the special *broadcast* address. This is an address on a network that forwards messages to *all* hosts on the network. There is no legitimate reason someone outside your network will need to broadcast to all your hosts. Configure your firewall and routers to block any packets directed to the broadcast address. Likewise, there is no reason people on your network should be sending packets to the broadcast address of *another* network. Block outgoing packets destined for the broadcast address.

Finally, not all addresses are valid Internet addresses. If you have set up a home network, you may have used an address starting with 192.168. The class C address block 192.168.0.0/16 is a private address block; these addresses are never assigned to a host on the Internet. Likewise, 10.0.0.0/8 and 172.16.0.0/12 are class A and class B, respectively, private address blocks. Do not allow incoming or outgoing packets with either a source or destination address from one of these address blocks.[T] There are special-use address ranges to avoid, too.[U] For example, 127.0.0.0/8 is reserved for the "loopback" address, used by a network interface to refer to itself. A list of addresses to block is given in Table 1.1.

[S]See the CERT "Handbook for computer security incident response teams (CSIRTS)," available on the Web at the time of writing at www.cert.org/archive/pdf/csirt-handbook.pdf.
[T]These address blocks are defined in RFC-1918.
[U]See RFC-3330.

Table 1.1 Addresses not on the Internet

Address	Use
0.0.0.0/32	See RFC-1700.
10.0.0.0/8	Private network addresses, as per RFC-1918.
127.0.0.0/8	Loopback addresses, as per RFC-1700.
169.254.0.0/16	"Link local" block. These addresses are typically assigned when another address cannot be obtained, such as when DHCP fails.
172.16.0.0/12	Private network addresses, as per RFC-1918.
192.0.2.0/24	Test network addresses. These addresses are for use in example code or documentation.
192.88.99.0/24	These addresses are reserved for relay anycast. See RFC-3068.
192.168.0.0/16	Private network addresses, as per RFC-1918.
192.18.0.0/15	Reserved for benchmarking tests of network devices, as per RFC-2544.
224.0.0.0/4	Reserved for IPv4 multicast. See RFC-3171.
240.0.0.0/4	The original class E address space is still reserved. This includes the special address 255.255.255.255 used for limited broadcast. See RFC-1700.

DDoS Appliances

DDoS appliances are network hardware with specialized firmware to detect anomalous network traffic and divert or drop that traffic to mitigate a DDoS attack. Many models also offer screening of *outbound* traffic, so that you aren't the source of a DDoS attack. Cisco Systems, Inc,[V] RioRey, Inc.,[W] Top Layer Security, Inc.,[X] and others sell DDoS appliances.

These appliances rely on detecting anomalous network traffic. While it is easy for legitimate users to generate legitimate-looking traffic, automatically generated traffic tends to have statistical characteristics that make it easier to spot. As a simple example, if your server is receiving a series of requests for a login from a particular host, all faster than any human could type, this traffic is probably part of a DDoS attack and can be dropped.

This approach has limits. If you know the method used to detect the anomalous traffic, you can work around it and still achieve the desired effect. For example, with more machines you can send requests to log in more slowly from each machine, but maintain the same overall rate. One way to do this is to simply purchase your victim's DDoS appliance, or network monitoring software, install it, and then craft your attack so that it is not detected. Despite these limits, deploying software or hardware to detect and block DDoS traffic can prevent many DDoS attacks.

[V] www.cisco.com/
[W] www.riorey.com/
[X] www.toplayer.com/

IDS/IPS Systems

IDS observes traffic on a port and attempts to match it against known patterns corresponding to malware, port scanning, or DDoS attacks. A well-known open-source IDS is Snort.[Y] Figure 1.4 shows the ACID Web interface to the Snort database. When Snort matches a pattern, it triggers an alert and can notify system administrators immediately. Additionally, it captures and logs traffic, which can help determine precisely what is happening.

EasyIDS is built around Snort and a few other tools, and packaged as a Linux distribution based on CentOS. It is installed on a single dedicated machine with two network interface cards (one facing the Internet, one facing your local network) to protect a network. This simplifies the installation, configuration, and maintenance of a network IDS (NIDS).

Bro is another open-source IDS.[Z] Bro relies heavily on protocol analysis to detect abnormal traffic, while Snort relies on a simple signature-based matching. Both Bro and Snort can be used together, as they are complementary and they have the capability to execute actions when they detect an event of interest. For example, if your IDS detects that a host is scanning ports on your machine, it might write a rule to your firewall or router to block the scanning host's address. The use of an IDS to actively

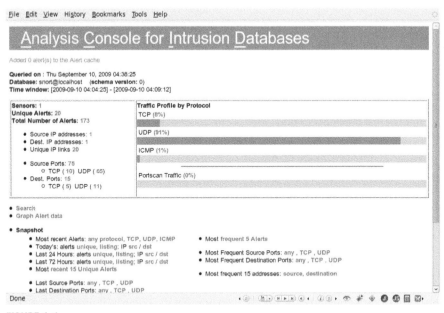

FIGURE 1.4

Displaying Intrusion Detection Data with ACID

[Y]www.snort.org/
[Z]www.bro-ids.org/

respond to intrusion attempts and block them transforms this system into one known as an intrusion prevention system (IPS).

Another strategy for detecting intrusion attempts is to create a *honeypot*. A honeypot is a carefully monitored machine or address that is used only to detect attacks. Normal, legitimate traffic is never directed to the honeypot machine, so any traffic that is detected at the honeypot is likely malicious traffic. Thus, by monitoring the honeypot, an IDS can detect when a network intrusion is being attempted. A simple example of a honeypot is an e-mail address created for the sole purpose of collecting spam. Since the e-mail address does not go to any legitimate recipient, any e-mail that arrives at the address is spam, and should be filtered from the rest of the e-mail. Project Honey Pot uses exactly this technique to monitor spammers.[AA]

Reacting to DDoS Attacks

Once a DDoS attack is underway, you have several options. You can attempt to block the hosts generating the traffic. Because of spoofing and the large number of hosts used in a DDoS attack, this may be difficult.

To block hosts, you must first identify them. If you are running an IDS, you will already have a list of addresses provided by the tool. Otherwise, you have to capture network traffic and analyze it. To capture network traffic, you can use tcpdump.[BB] This is a packet *sniffer* that can observe and record network traffic on an interface.

In the following example, we capture 1,000 packets using tcpdump.

```
$ tcpdump -c 1000 -w record.tcp eth0
tcpdump: listening on eth0, link-type EN10MB (Ethernet), capture
   size 96 bytes
1000 packets captured
1000 packets received by filter
0 packets dropped by kernel
```

An easier way to analyze network traffic is to use an actual network traffic analyzer, such as Wireshark.[CC] Wireshark is available for most platforms and is relatively easy to use. Figure 1.5 shows packets captured using Wireshark.

It is also possible to configure some routers to provide this information. Cisco routers, for instance, keep a total of the number of times each rule is matched. In the following, we create a rule to match echo and one to match echo reply (pings).

```
access-list 169 permit icmp any any echo
access-list 169 permit icmp any any echo-reply
```

Including *log-input* at the end of a rule will also create a log of matching network traffic. Use *show log* to see the log. We can now get the number of times each rule is matched via the *show access-list* command, which gives the number of times each rule is matched by network traffic.

[AA]http://projecthoneypot.org/
[BB]While tcpdump is common on UNIX and Linux machines, on Windows you can use WinDump, an open-source clone of tcpdump.
[CC]www.wireshark.org/

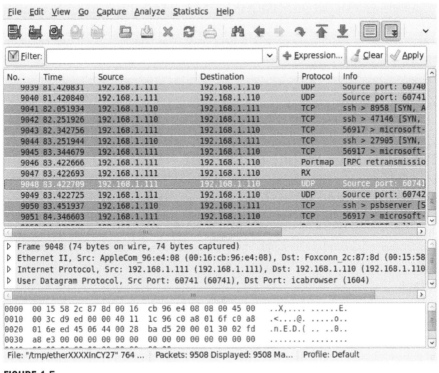

FIGURE 1.5

Wireshark

If you are being subjected to a ping flood or some other type of DDoS attack using a particular kind of traffic, one approach is to *rate limit* that kind of traffic. Rate limiting sets a limit as to the amount of bandwidth a particular kind of traffic can consume. When the threshold is exceeded, packets are simply dropped. This solves the problem of a ping flood, but if the DDoS traffic looks like legitimate traffic this may not be an option.[DD]

Over-Provisioning and Adaptive Provisioning

The DDoS attack will only succeed if it can overwhelm your network bandwidth or your servers. One way to prevent a DDoS attack is simply to increase your network and server capacity beyond what is necessary for legitimate traffic. This extra capability can be brought online if a DDoS attack is detected. This *over-provisioning* can be expensive, however.

[DD]*Network Security Technologies and Solutions (CCIE Professional Development Series)* by Yusuf Bhaiji, Cisco Press, 2008, discusses how to properly configure routers to filter or throttle ICMP traffic. The United States National Security Agency (NSA) also publishes guides to router security configuration. See www.nsa.gov/ia/guidance/security_configuration_guides/.

An alternative if you use an ISP is to purchase additional capacity for the duration of the DDoS attack. This adaptive provisioning can be provided via *burstable circuits*, which can carry additional capacity if necessary. You typically pay a rate based on your *average* use of the connection. Since attackers often "tune" the attack while it is in progress, you will still need to carefully monitor the attack to determine how best to respond. For example, an attack may change from trying to overload a server to exploiting a network protocol.

THE FUTURE OF DENIAL OF SERVICE

Malware is now big business, and operating botnets has become a source of significant income. Developing a large botnet is a financial investment. Likewise, considerable economic activity is moving onto the Internet, with some companies completely dependent on the Internet for their business, including Google and Amazon.com. All this creates a marketplace to supply more advanced attack and defense capabilities.

Attack

Based in St. Petersburg, the Russian Business Network (RBN) is a hosting organization that offers "bulletproof" hosting and a variety of other services, including botnet rental, so you don't even need to create your own botnet.[EE] If you can lease time on an existing botnet, and use it effectively for a DDoS attack, you have successfully reduced a technical challenge to a simple matter of paying some money.

This is probably the shape of the future in DDoS. Creating and controlling a large botnet is still somewhat challenging, and also presents legal risks. It is also the case that botnets can be "hijacked" if someone else, perhaps another criminal enterprise, gets access to the command and control channels.

Current trends show that the malware world is becoming less vertically integrated and more specialized. Many components of successful malware are not, by themselves, illegal. It is thus perfectly reasonable to set up shop and develop and sell software to enable DDoS attacks, so long as the software has a potential legal application, as well. For example, software used to protect intellectual property and thwart reverse engineering can also be used to harden malware against reverse engineering, making it hard to discover just what a particular kind of malware is doing, and how to counteract it. Digital rights management (DRM) techniques can cloak a malware payload until the time arrives to launch a DDoS attack. While the tools to conduct a DDoS attack are improving, fortunately so are the tools to defend against an attack.

[EE]RBN is the originator of the MPack malware kit, which you can purchase for between $500 and $1000 (at the time of writing). Included with this kit is technical support and regular updates to the vulnerabilities it can exploit. Additional functionality can be purchased to target specific vulnerabilities or to cloak the software against antimalware and antivirus programs. MPack includes a Web-based management console to allow you to track its progress as it infects machines.

Defense

One possibility may be to structure the defense in the same way as the offense. By connecting several nodes using peer-to-peer networks and exchanging data about network traffic, it may be possible to automatically detect and mitigate DDoS attacks in real time.[FF]

Even if one is correctly filtering the malicious traffic from a DDoS attack a network segment may become overloaded, since the filtering is being done locally. By adding additional layers of protocol to the Internet it may be possible to distribute the defense against a DDoS attack. In this case when a DDoS attack is detected, information about the attack is pushed back so that routers close to the attack sources perform the filtering. This effectively distributes the defense against the attack by recruiting routers near the sources.[GG]

Right now a key aspect of DDoS is that it is computationally easy to generate the traffic. One potential way to make DDoS harder is to impose additional overhead on the originator of the traffic. This approach uses "puzzles" that must be solved before a connection is allowed. This reduces the rate at which attack sources can generate traffic, and reduces the overall effectiveness of the DDoS attack.

One approach that has been proposed for dealing with DDoS extortion is to legally require companies to report both threats and attacks to law enforcement, and to impose severe penalties for not reporting. The idea is that forcing these attacks into the open and involving law enforcement early raises the stakes for would-be extortionists.

SUMMARY

This chapter showed you that DDoS attacks can do significant harm. By recruiting many machines into a botnet and directing a flood of traffic against a victim, one can overwhelm the victim and degrade, deny, or in some cases even destroy the service. We explained what DoS and DDoS attacks are and how a DDoS attack is launched, as well as providing an understanding of why DDos attacks are so hard to defend against. However, you should also have the capability of building a defensive strategy based on the framework of tools and methods that we discussed.

Endnotes

1. Richards J. Denial of service: the Estonian Cyberwar and its implications for U.S. national security. Int Aff Rev 2009; 18(1).
2. Clayton R. The rising tide: DDoS by defective designs and defaults. Proceedings of the 2nd Conference on Steps to Reducing Unwanted Traffic on the Internet (SRUTI'06). Berkeley, California; 2006.

[FF]For one such approach see Guangsen Zhang and Manish Parashar, "Cooperative Defence Against DDoS Attacks," *Journal of Research and Practice in Information Technology*, vol. 38, no. 1, 2006.
[GG]See Katerina Argyraki and David Cheriton, "Active Internet Traffic Filtering: Real-Time Response to Denial of Service Attacks," presented at the USENIX Annual Technical Conference, 2005.

War Dialing

2

INFORMATION IN THIS CHAPTER

- How War Dialing Attacks Work
- The Danger of War Dialing
- The Future of War Dialing
- Defenses against War Dialing

It's the mid-1990s and the Internet boom is really getting underway; however, high-speed "always-on" connections are extremely expensive, and neither cable nor phone companies are providing home service as of yet. In this era before being hardwired into the Internet was a standard idea, the way people connected to networks was by utilizing devices called *modems*. Modems connect to a computer on one side and the standard analog telephone system on the other side. This allows users to use a modem connected to their computer to "dial in" to a network by calling a modem that is connected to that network and set to answer.

> **NOTE**
>
> The term modem is an abbreviated combination of the words "modulation" and "demodulation." Modulation is the process of encoding a digital signal into an analog signal. Demodulation is the reverse of modulation and used to encode an analog signal into a digital signal.

As with many innovations, private and public entities looked for ways to use the technology to save money. NYNEX was the regional telephone company for New England that resulted from the breakup of Bell Telephone in the mid-1980s. Like many companies, NYNEX saw the value in the idea of using modems to allow technicians to remotely connect to their systems for maintenance purposes. Unfortunately, the added convenience this brought also created opportunities for others.

Jester was an underage teen who also had a modem and enjoyed playing around on the networks he could find. He utilized his modem to dial a range of numbers until he identified modems that he could connect to, a process known as *war dialing*. This term came from the title of the 1983 movie *War Games* in which Matthew Broderick's character utilizes a modem to dial a series of numbers looking for modems to connect to and ultimately almost destroys the world. At some point, Jester found the NYNEX modem connected to communications equipment servicing the community of Rutland, Massachusetts, and the Worcester Airport.[1]

Unfortunately, for the people of Rutland and anyone trying to use the airport on March 10, 1997, Jester defeated the security of the computer the modem was connected to and used his access to shut down the entire loop carrier system. In turn, this blacked out the telephone service for the community and all communication at the airport, including the system that allowed aircraft to activate the runway lights before landing, for about six hours. Obviously, this was a big deal for both the phone company and the government who went after Jester (so nicknamed because that is what he changed the system identification to) and led to one of the first prosecutions of a juvenile for hacking.

The use of Internet-based connectivity to internal networks using virtual private network (VPN), rather than directly dialing into the network over a private line, has become the standard way that users remotely connect to networks today. This standard operating procedure has steadily removed the need for organizations to use modems within their own networks on a massive scale and instead limits their use to unique devices that provide a very specific value to the person who implemented it. The value could be that the organization or a vendor requires a modem to be directly connected to a device as a redundant method to access it or simply for access to legacy systems that do not have access to broadband connections.

It may be counterintuitive, but the fact modems are utilized less and less in modern organizations can actually make them more dangerous. In the late 1990s, the publicizing of the prosecutions of Jester (as well as others, such as members of the "Legion of Doom"[A]) and the depiction of attackers on TV and in movies such as *Hackers* and *The Net* made organizations aware of the security concerns associated with attaching modems to their networks. This drove most organizations to focus on the security of the systems connected to these devices.

Because modems are much less pervasive, attackers and defenders focus much more attention on subverting and protecting firewalls or other perimeter devices. This reduced focus means it is much more likely that organizations will not put the proper security in place for modems (or even know they exist in the network) because "nobody attacks them anymore." Not securing a device because nobody is looking for it is known as *security through obscurity* and is not security at all.

[A]http://online.wsj.com/article/SB124136230988580795.html

EPIC FAIL

Securing modems and other services by simply attempting to hide them from casual view is a poor methodology to consider. Although it is a good idea to implement defensive measures that follow the concept of security through obscurity, it is not wise to make this the only defensive measure in place. This defensive measure assumes that flaws will not be found because malicious attackers will not be able to find them. However, over history the actual effectiveness of this method has proven to fail in many cases.

An example of security through obscurity is hiding the advertisement of a wireless network that has been implemented for private use only. Many administrators will configure wireless networks to prevent broadcasting their existence; however, most wireless hacking tools today still identify the networks very quickly. Hence, the concept of hiding the wireless network as a primary means of security will not be sufficient to protect the network.

We can still consider using security through obscurity as one of the pieces of the final solution. Adding other controls such as address filtering, WPA2 encryption, back-end authentication, and wireless intrusion detection controls can hinder the progress of attackers. Think of it like this: each control is another speed bump the attacker will have to circumvent, and adding more speed bumps will decrease the speed the attacker can compromise a network. Security through obscurity is a good speed bump, but it is far from being a stop sign.

Modems are not totally gone from today's networks. Organizations still use dial-up connectivity for administration of network devices, supporting legacy network implementations, and even employee remote access where high-speed connections are still unavailable or too expensive. This means that war dialing may result in fewer responses than in the 1980s and 1990s, but the opportunities are still there.

HOW WAR DIALING ATTACKS WORK

Attackers and penetration testers perform war dialing attacks to identify telephone numbers directly connected to modems. A war dialing attack consists of several steps that may ultimately allow complete access to otherwise secured network resources. Some of the goals of war dialing attacks may be to obtain network access achieved by circumventing weak controls or identifying poorly implemented communication channels that can be leveraged by an attacker for the purpose of toll fraud activities.

Attacks focused on a specific target require the attacker to identify a range of telephone numbers belonging to the target. This information can be found using a wide range of sources, including the telephone book crammed in the bottom drawer of your nightstand. Random attacks will usually consist of attackers scanning large blocks of numbers in an effort to locate any numbers connected to live modems.

> **WARNING**
>
> It is common for attackers to compromise systems that have no direct ties to the real target. These unrelated compromised systems can be used against the target solely for hiding the identity of the true attacker or can also be used to amplify the power of the attack against the real target. As related to a wartime scenario, we can think of these compromised systems as "collateral damage." They are not the primary target, but they are serving a purpose.
>
> For instance, let us assume that the attacker wants to attack our favorite neighborhood electronics retailer, "Buy More." Instead of going toe-to-toe and attacking the retailer directly, the attacker will most likely conduct attacks from systems that cannot be tied directly back to him or her (certainly our attacker wants to reduce the chances of being sent to the state penitentiary). The attacker can compromise many other systems with poor security postures first and then use those systems to "pivot" off or proxy the attack, making it appear the attack came from a totally different source.
>
> In some cases, attacks may appear to be coming from entirely different countries. When dealing with tracing the source of an attack, it is very difficult to get people within the same legal jurisdiction to work together. Now, imagine trying to get international cooperation if an attack appears to be sourced from different countries alltogether. These types of attacks make it significantly harder to track down the attacker. However, even though our attacker is using a pivot attack, caution should still be taken, or the risk of getting caught is still very real.

Gathering Numbers for War Dialing

The attacks may be attempted against a single number, a block of numbers assigned to a company, or an entire exchange of telephone numbers. The scope of the attack and the amount of numbers dialed will depend on the attackers' goal. Regardless of the total number of phone numbers dialed, the goal remains the same; identify telephone numbers that may provide an attacker alternate points of entry into a network or system.

If a specific target is the goal of an attacker, the first task that needs to be completed is to build a list of telephone numbers owned by the organization. This can be accomplished by a variety of ways, and sometimes the simplest methods of information gathering will provide the desired results.

One obvious place for attackers to look while building a list of telephone numbers is the Web site of the organization the attacker is targeting. An important thing to remember here is that businesses want to sell you their product, and generally this means they are not trying to hide from legitimate consumers. Visiting the organization's Web site and its "contact us" or "support" links will likely provide attackers with a list of telephone numbers to start with or at least provide the attacker with information about the blocks of telephone numbers the organization uses.

Another popular method of obtaining telephone numbers is using various online resources that may provide telephone number information not traditionally listed on the main corporate Web site. One resource that provides helpful information is the "whois" service provided by InterNIC,[B] as well as domain registrar's sites such as

---

[B]www.internic.net/

Network Solutions[C] and GoDaddy.[D] This service allows attackers to obtain information about administrative and technical contacts and usually several valid telephone numbers belonging to an organization. An example of the type of information gathered from one of these resources is displayed below:

```
Registrant:
Hometown Business USA
One Fake Address Plaza
Port Jefferson Station, NY 11776
US

Domain Name: ICHDONTHINKSO.COM

Administrative Contact:
Admin@ICHDONTTHINKSO.COM
One Fake Address Plaza
Port Jefferson Station, NY 11776
US
Phone: 631-555-1234 fax: 631-555-1288

Technical Contact:
Tech@ICHDONTTHINKSO.COM
One Fake Address Plaza
Port Jefferson Station, NY 11776
US
Phone: 631-555-1235 fax: 631-555-1289

Record expires on 13-May-2020.
Record created on 12-May-2005.
Database last updated on 23-Aug-2009 20:11:13 EDT.
```

Sweeping for Live Modems

Once the attacker has performed some research and has gathered phone numbers, the real fun begins. Loading the phone numbers into a war dialing program and waiting to see the results is one of the most interesting and fruitful parts of the attack. While conducting war dialing attacks, the attacker may observe several different types of responses from the war dialing software, depending on what types of answers are received from the numbers dialed. Additionally, if large blocks or telephone numbers are scanned, it may take quite some time to complete dialing all the numbers, depending on how many modems and lines are used by the attacker. Most of the existing war dialing software provides support for performing war dialing attacks with multiple modems at the same time. Additionally, the use of some Voice over Internet Protocol (VoIP) war dialers let attackers use a large number of lines to perform war dialing with minimal configuration changes. The more modems an attacker can use, the less overall time will be needed to dial large blocks of telephone numbers.

[C]www.networksolutions.com
[D]www.godaddy.com

NOTE

While war dialing, an attacker may decide to dial entire exchanges in search of listening modems. Our example list happens to be some of the exchanges dialed in the movie *WarGames*.[2]

311-555-0000	311-399-0000
311-555-0001	311-399-0001
311-555-0002	311-399-0002
311-555-0003	311-399-0003
...	...
311-555-9996	311-399-9996
311-555-9997	311-399-9997
311-555-9998	311-399-9998
311-555-9999	311-399-9999

Note: The number for the W.O.P.R. computer modem in *WarGames* was 311-399-2364. We will save you some time; the password is "Joshua," but please do not start a game of Global Thermonuclear War.

Modem Reply Types

Much like when a person picks up a phone and dials a telephone number, the expected response is to hear a person answer the phone call. This is not always the case, as I am sure most of us have experienced calling a number and expecting to hear a person but instead being greeted by the annoying screeching of a FAX machine. Most war dialing software has the capability of detecting several different types of call responses and can provide details and statistics based on the number of calls attempted. A few of the call response statuses are described below.

- **Carrier.** Telephone numbers classified as carrier lines means end-to-end connectivity is possible for data exchange. For the sake of the context of this chapter, we will refer to a carrier line as one that is connected to a modem.
- **Tone.** A telephone number that is dialed and classified as tone may be of interest for attackers who are interested in performing toll fraud attacks. In these cases, it may be possible for attackers who detect tone lines to dial into the number and then make an outbound call from that number. Imagine an attacker calling into a line with tone enabled and then making long-distance calls to friends in Germany. Whom do you think is stuck with the bill?
- **Voice.** Advanced modems have the capabilities of detecting a human voice or voicemail system. Telephone numbers identified as voice or voicemail are usually classified as a voice system and pose little threat, as they are most likely not directly connected to a modem.
- **Busy.** This category consists of telephone numbers that were busy during the initial war dialing attempt. The numbers identified as busy can be manually dialed after the completion of the test. Some war dialing software will tag the telephone number as busy and attempt to redial the number again at the end of the test.

- **FAX.** As many businesses still rely on fax machines, most modems and war dialing programs are capable of detecting and classifying fax lines.
- **Timeout.** In the event a number is dialed and no response is received or detected by the war dialing software, the software may indicate it had experienced a timeout for the number.

War Dialing Tools

Some of the tools that attackers use today have been around for many years and are still used because of the quality, reliability, and ease of use of the tool. Efficiency and accuracy are important parts of war dialing attacks, and thus many great tools have been developed to help automate and record results for attacks that are performed.

ToneLoc

This DOS application programmed in C is the creation of Minor Threat & Mucho Mass. The program was released in 1994 and derives its name from "Tone Locator." This application was one of the most used war dialing programs in its day and is still used by war dialers today. The source code[E] for ToneLoc was released to the public several years ago, and user manuals[F] are still very easy to find.

THC-SCAN

THC-SCAN was originally released in 1995, and the current release is at version 2.0.1. The current release was published in 2005 and was updated to offer support for newer operating systems. The logging capabilities and ease of configuration of THC-SCAN make this a great choice for a low-cost open-source war dialing application. The source code and documentation for THC-SCAN are still available at the THC Web site.[G] The test setup used during the development of this book included THC-SCAN 2.0.1 installed on Windows Vista using a USB-to-serial cable connected to an AOpen FM56EXV external serial modem. Amazingly enough, the entire investment was less than $15.00 to set up, thanks to a local Goodwill store.

Several utility programs come with THC-SCAN, making the initial setup of this war dialing software fairly painless. MOD-DET.exe is a Windows executable file used to help detect modems that are connected to the computer. If a modem is detected, the MOD-DET.exe application will provide information that will be needed for the next step in setting up the computer for war dialing. In particular, the information about the COM port, interrupt request (IRQ) number, and base address the modem is assigned will be required. Figure 2.1 illustrates the information gathered while setting up the war dialer in our test environment.

Once the information needed to configure THC-SCAN is obtained, the next step is to use the TS-CFG.exe application to prepare the THC-SCAN configuration files,

---

[E]www.oldskoolphreak.com/etc/TL110SRC.ZIP
[F]www.textfiles.com/hacking/tl-user.txt
[G]http://freeworld.thc.org/thc-scan/

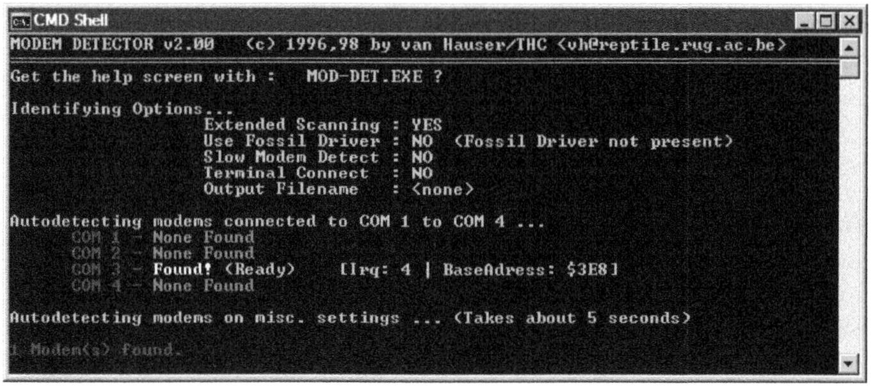

FIGURE 2.1

Detecting the Modem for Configuration

so the software can use the modem for war dialing. In our test environment, we simply changed the COM port, IRQ, and base address to match what was detected when MOD-DET.exe was run.

In addition to the options discussed, several other options can be modified, depending on what type of environment the war dialing attack is being conducted from. One commonly configured option is the "dial prefix." This option is sometimes modified when the modem first needs to dial an initial series of numbers before being provided access to an outside line. For instance, if the number 8 needs to be dialed to access an outside line, an attacker would modify the dial prefix to dial the number 8 before dialing other numbers. Figure 2.2 illustrates the configuration screen that TS-CNF.exe provides.

Figure 2.3 illustrates the THC-SCAN interface as it begins a test war dial. The information provided within the command shell is verbose and provides good visual feedback on the progress of the scan. Some of the information provided includes the number of calls made and how many are left, as well as the reply types from the numbers that were tested.

Information from the war dial is also logged to a series of files for review after the scan is completed. THC-SCAN is a good tool for war dialing and has proven its worth over many years.

PhoneSweep

PhoneSweep by Sandstorm Enterprises[H] is a commercial war dialer that provides many of the same benefits as some of the previously mentioned tools. The application is easy to use and supports multiple modems for outbound calls, which

---

[H]www.sandstorm.net/

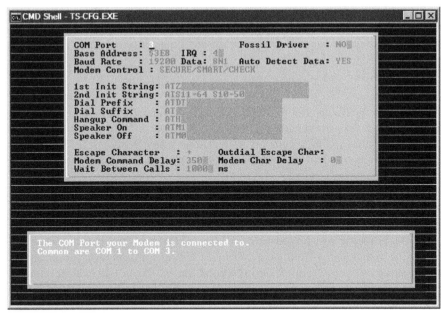

FIGURE 2.2

Configuring the Modem

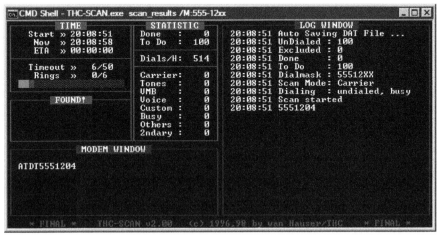

FIGURE 2.3

Viewing the THC-SCAN Statistics and Progress

can drastically reduce overall scan time for larger assessments. PhoneSweep also has detection capabilities that allow it to identify over 470 types of dialed systems, as well as the capability to perform dictionary attacks[I] against identified systems.

WarVOX

The crew over at Metasploit[J] has done a great job with extending the capabilities of war dialing with the release of WarVOX. This war dialing tool is a Ruby on Rails[K] applications, which runs on a standalone Ruby WEBrick HTTP server.[L] The most fascinating part of this tool is that it performs war dialing attacks without using a traditional modem.

WarVOX classifies dialed numbers by analyzing the actual audio from the calls. This allows attackers the ability of determining the type and classification of the responses from the numbers dialed. Another interesting aspect about WarVOX is that it will record each call for offline analysis. Attackers can listen to the actual audio from each call made and use information gleaned from the recordings for future attacks. Figure 2.4 shows the visual feedback on the number of calls attempted and the classification of the numbers analyzed within WarVOX.

Several types of telephone numbers were tested during the writing of this book, and all numbers tested were classified correctly. Initial setup of the WarVOX tool and service provider configuration took approximately 25 minutes (this includes the time it took to register an account with our VoIP service provider). Our test setup included Fedora 10, WarVOX version 1.0.1, and one of the service providers recommended in the WarVOX project documentation. The ease of setup, configuration, and initiation of war dialing attacks makes WarVOX a valuable tool for attackers and penetration testers alike.

Table 2.1 provides a quick reference to some of the war dialer software this chapter has covered, as well as some other alternatives.

[I]Given an encrypted password there are many different ways to proceed. A brute force attack is an exhaustive attack that literally tries every possible variation of characters, numbers, and symbols until the attack results in the discovery of the clear text password. Constraints can be put in place to narrow the scope of the attack based on implementation of specific considerations such as maximum or minimum password length. A dictionary attack tries all likely passwords from a list. The list may be much shorter and resemble the type of works you may find in a dictionary. For this reason, this type of attack usually requires less time to perform and is more of a focused effort. If a user has chosen a dictionary word or a common password, a dictionary attack will usually provide positive results in much less time compared to brute force methods. "Clever" (but common) variations of words can also be part of the dictionaries, such as "pa55w0rd".

[J]www.metasploit.com/

[K]http://rubyonrails.org/

[L]www.webrick.com/

FIGURE 2.4

Viewing the WarVOX Scan Analysis

Table 2.1 War dialing tools	
WarVOX	ToneLoc
THC-SCAN	ModemScan
TeleSweep	iWAR
ShokDial	Telescan

THE DANGER OF WAR DIALING

Modems can cause organizations to incur significant risk if best practices are not implemented during their deployment and use. Although there has been a decline in the use of modems for legacy connectivity, the threat is still very real. Penetration tests still reveal a significant amount of modems of which many have been implemented to provide organizations a solution for administration or remote access. However, there are still cases where administrators need to hunt down rogue modems implemented without the knowledge of the Information Technology (IT) department.

Out-of-Band Support Channels

Although many network administrators have moved as far away from dial-up access as possible, there still exists a need to implement modems for communications for a variety of situations. One of the most frequent implementations encountered involves using modems as an out-of-band communications solution for managing network equipment such as routers and switches. Out-of-band communications provide administrators the capability of remotely managing devices should traditional local area network or wide area network connectivity become unreliable or unavailable.

Although modems may be implemented for the purpose of out-of-band communications, poor implementation of such devices may provide an avenue of attack allowing attackers to gain access to the core backbone of the network. If an attacker is able to connect to a router via a poorly secured modem and successfully authenticate, there are many type of attacks that can be performed that may reduce the confidentiality, integrity, and availability of the network and the data that passes through it.

If an attacker has appropriate access, he or she may set new passwords for the router, essentially hijacking the device. Administrators may have a difficult time reclaiming administrative access to the router, depending on whether or not physical access to the router is required to regain control. This may take a considerable amount of time if the network administrators are not prepared. Additionally, many network administrators fail to implement proper logging for failed logon events, which allows attackers to perform extensive dictionary or brute-force attacks without detection. Successful authentication attacks may allow attackers to maintain access for long periods without detection by administrators. Once this level of access is achieved, the attacker can cripple the entire network by reconfiguring the router.

Attackers may use router software to sniff network traffic as it passes through the router. This obviously is a great concern, as many network administrators fail to implement encrypted protocols. Sniffing network traffic can also provide attackers with a wealth of information about the protocols and the types of traffic that traverses the network. This type of attack will most likely allow attackers to sniff legitimate usernames and passwords, allowing for further attacks against services available on the network.

The attacker may be able to perform denial-of-service (DoS) attacks, as explained in Chapter 1, "Denial of Service," by configuring the router to route all traffic to a nonexistent address, also known as a *null route* or *black hole*. This of course will cause a total loss of data, as it traverses this point within the network.

Remote access for out-of-band communications should be secured to prevent these types of attacks. The previous attacks described only account for a small amount of what an attacker can do if modems connected to support devices are compromised.

Unauthorized Employee Access

One of the oldest war dialing attack scenarios deals with an employee who must have access to his or her work desktop computer while he or she is away from the office. Unfortunately, sometimes employees who are trying to do good deeds for the organization can unknowingly introduce vulnerabilities that weaken the organization's security posture.

In this scenario, our technically savvy sales manager purchases a modem from his or her favorite electronics retailer and installs the modem in his or her work computer without the approval of the IT department and without consulting the organization's remote access policies. Thanks to the ease of installation of hardware components and software installation wizards, this task is simple to complete. All the salesperson needs to do now is connect the FAX line or any other spare phone line to his or her modem and he or she is ready to dial-in from his or her home computer.

Why is this type of access dangerous? Implementing modems should be closely scrutinized by IT employees and must be controlled. Poorly implemented devices may allow anyone to connect to the modem and thus the organization's internal network. Once successful authentication to the modem is performed, the remote access may not only allow access to the computer but likely allow access to the entire network the computer has. An attacker may be able to gain unrestricted access to the internal network and be able to do so without ever passing through a firewall or VPN device.

Vendor Support Modems

Many hardware and software vendors offer support services to customers who purchase and implement their products. For example, many building environmental control systems such as heating, ventilation, and air-conditioning (HVAC) can now be managed and serviced remotely. This provides a tremendous value to building management personnel and the companies that support service and regular maintenance of the system.

Some vendors require dial-up or network access to the equipment installed as part of the service level agreement (SLA) for a support contract. This provides the vendor with the appropriate access required to troubleshoot problems and perform upgrades as required by the SLA.

As an example, you may be able to see how an attacker can connect to a modem used to manage a HVAC system and gain unauthorized access to building environmental controls. This type of attack can allow attackers to cause serious disruption to the workflow of an organization. Imagine sitting in your office and the building temperature being raised to 85 degrees and not a Piña Colada machine in sight! Even worse, imagine the attacker shutting off the cooling to your data center. Additionally, if the control system is connected to the network, the attacker may be able to traverse the connection to the control and gain access to network resources. Compound this with the premise that most networks are not properly segregated and you now have a recipe for disaster.

THE FUTURE OF WAR DIALING

The methods discussed within this chapter are well established and not likely to change any time soon. However, the same thought process behind war dialing for modems is being repeated in many innovative ways and will continue to influence the way attackers look at things. The type of scanning discussed in Chapter 3, "Penetration 'Testing,'" follows the same general methodology as war dialing, only from a network perspective.

Instead of using a modem to dial phone numbers within an exchange, network scanners and penetration testing programs probe a series of Internet Protocol addresses within a range. Both war dialer and scanner software listen for specific responses from the target devices and then provide you with information regarding possible targets to attack. Another scanning approach actually derives its name from war dialing, and that is *war driving*.

War driving is a method used by attackers to discover wireless networks. Originally, the term was coined because attackers would drive around in their cars using wireless scanning software to find unsecured wireless networks. By finding an unsecured wireless network, an attacker has circumvented the perimeter security of the network in the same way finding an unsecured modem does. More information on war driving can be found in *WarDriving and Wireless Penetration Testing*[M] and *Kismet Hacking*.[N] You will also note that most of the actions mentioned in the section "Defenses against War Dialing" also have equivalents in wireless security.

Another way this attack methodology is being adapted is social war dialing or vishing. This is a combination of the use of "robo" or "auto" dialers and VoIP to call a series of numbers in a range and then use social engineering attacks to try to trick the person on the other end of the phone into giving out personal information. This type of attack is based on having control of the VoIP system the war dialer is utilizing so that the attacker can spoof the information the victim sees on his or her caller ID system.

Attacking using this method usually starts with identifying a small community with only a single local bank to increase the likelihood of success. The attacker then programs the VoIP system that he or she controls to display the name of the bank and a valid phone number for that bank. When someone answers the phone, the VoIP system plays a prerecorded message that states that the user's bank account has been compromised and the customer needs to change his or her PIN code to avoid charges to his or her account. The VoIP system then uses an automated menu to ask for and gather information such as account numbers, credit card numbers, and the victim's current PIN.

Since the caller ID shows what may be valid information for the victim's bank, this is a particularly effective attack for compromising someone's identity. Social war dialing continues to evolve as new technologies emerge. It is now being utilized to "auto text" messages to ranges of phone numbers owned by cell phone providers in attempts to trick a user into providing personal information to an attacker. This type of constant adaptation of the thought process behind war dialing shows that some version of it will be with us for a long time.

DEFENSES AGAINST WAR DIALING

The best defense against any type of attack is to eliminate the attack surface itself. In the case of war dialing, you can accomplish this if you are able to eliminate modems from your network. An attacker who war dials your phone exchange when

---

[M]*WarDriving and Wireless Penetration Testing*, ISBN: 978-1-59749-111-2 (Syngress)
[N]*Kismet Hacking*, ISBN: 978-1-59749-117-4 (Syngress)

no modems exist comes up empty and moves on (unless he or she is just trying to annoy you by randomly making your phones ring). For many different reasons, you may not be able to accomplish this, and even if you are able to, there is no guarantee that your network will stay modem-free. Therefore, you should put in place policies, procedures, and implementation strategies regarding the proper use of modems, even if modems do not currently exist in your environment.

Attack Surface Reduction

For many reasons, many organizations prefer the outright banning of modems. This does not mean that remote access can no longer occur, but rather it is more cost- effective to use a combination of the Internet and VPN access to provide this rather than the use of modems. Since VPNs have become the standard for remote access solutions in these organizations, the use of modems now represents a second perimeter that must be secured.

The banning of modems begins with setting company policies against the use of modems within the network. Written policies are only as good as your enforcement of those policies, however. For this reason, you should view the banning as a first step that also includes security testing to find modems (war dialing yourself) and a well-known penalty for anyone who adds a modem to your network in violation of your policy.

If it is not possible to ban modem use from your environment because some vendors still require them to support their equipment, then you should look at whether these vendors will ever use them without your knowledge. For example, your televisor robot has stopped working because its positronic brain is trying to resolve a conflict between the first law of robotics (a robot may not injure a human being or, through inaction, allow a human being to come to harm[3]) and allowing you to watch the latest installment of a VH1 reality TV series. The question is whether the support team from US Robots and Mechanical Men, Inc., would automatically detect this issue and dial in to the wireless support modem installed in your robot to correct the problem or whether this type of repair would only occur after a support call and with you on the phone.

If the manufacturer's support team would only connect with the malfunctioning device after you initiated the action, then there is no reason for you to leave the modem

---

TIP

The banning of modem access to your network is not always something that you can accomplish even in today's world. If you are completely based in the United States (or other countries) and have constant high-speed access to the Internet, then banning modems as a remote access solution is possible. In the Asia/Pacific countries, including Australia, this is not necessarily the case, and modems are still being used to connect to networks and work remotely.

Even in these areas of the world, you can still eliminate the attack surface from your network by removing your listening modems and requiring that all your users dial in to an Internet service provider then connect to your infrastructure using the Internet and VPN. However, this may not be cost-effective if this decision would require you to pay for your user's monthly Internet charges.

engaged during normal operations. Therefore, your policies and procedures surrounding this modem would require that the modem remain turned off, disconnected from the phone system, or set to dial out only during normal operations in order to reduce the attack surface. During an authorized support procedure, you would change the mode of operation of the modem, making it available for use by the manufacturer. In our example, you would disable the modem again after the US Robots support team has cleared the conflict. You should also follow their recommendation to avoid using a televisor robot for this type of programming and watch *Ninja Warrior* to get your reality TV fix instead.

Modem Hardening

Besides leaving modems disconnected or turned off when not specifically in use, you can harden modems by utilizing the logical access controls that are available within the modem settings themselves. Modems can be set to automatically return a call or "call back" a modem that is dialing into the network before allowing access to occur. This setting forces an attacker to provide a legitimate phone number for a modem he or she is using and provides investigators information that can be used while attempting to identify the source of an attempted or successful breach. You can also define a list of authorized phone numbers that the modem will accept calls from. Although this setting will still allow spoofing to occur, an attacker must first figure out what the legitimate phone numbers are.

System Hardening

An attacker does not get access to your network just because his or her modem negotiates a connection with yours. After connecting, the attacker must provide a valid logon to the system the modem is connected to. Insuring that this login is as strong as possible is therefore very important. Regardless of the system that the modem is connected to, the login should be integrated with your normal authentication mechanisms for your environment rather than just a local login. This ensures that all the standard password policies around format and complexity are integrated. In addition, you are

---

NOTE

The two main types of authentication services that are available to for authorizing access to your network through a modem are Remote Access Dial-In User Service (RADIUS) and Terminal Access Controller Access Control System Plus (TACACS+). RADIUS is an open specification defined in RFC 2865[O] and is utilized extensively even though it is not as secure at TACACS+. The TACACS+ specification is a protocol defined by Cisco, which makes it proprietary rather than open, but is available for use with non-Cisco devices, including Windows-based systems.

[O]www.ietf.org/rfc/rfc2865.txt?number =2865

able to integrate the removal of these logins into your standard processes for removing access for people who no longer need it.

You should also ensure logins that give you access through modems are configured to lockout (at least for a period of time) after a few failed attempts. As we mentioned in the section "Scenario 1: Out-of-Band Support Channels," one of the methods that attackers employ is to use brute-force dictionary attacks against the login page for the modem. If an account locks out after only three failed attempts, even if this lockout is only for 30 seconds at a time, it effectively defeats this type of attack (although it does also provide attackers with a way to create a DoS condition).

In addition to the requirement for strong authentication mechanisms, system hardening includes configuring logging and alerting mechanisms. The most important items to log are outgoing calls (this relates to requiring "call back" as described in the section "Modem Hardening"), successful and failed authentication attempts, and account lockouts. Finally, you must keep in mind that all modems represent a network edge, and therefore, any system that has a modem attached should have a firewall between that system and the rest of your internal network.

Discovery

As we discussed in the section "Scenario 2: Unauthorized Employee Access," it is easy for an employee to set up a rogue modem within your environment. The only way to know no one has done this is to perform self-testing using the same war dialing software that an attacker might (see the section "War Dialing Tools" for specific software that you can use for self-testing). The best way to set up this self-testing is to schedule a war dialing scan of your entire range of valid numbers for each night. Returns from these scans should be integrated with your logging or alerting infrastructure, and any nonauthorized modems should generate an alert to a security administrator.

Another even more in-depth idea is to try to set up a "honeypot" to try to catch possible attackers without exposing your real resources to these attackers. Sandstorm Enterprises, whose PhoneSweep product was discussed in the section "War Dialing Tools," has a product named *Sandtrap* that allows you to set up a modem (or use a modem that is already in use) to attract an attacker and record his or her actions. This includes allowing him or her to operate in a simulated environment in order to provide law enforcement with evidence of an attempted breach of your environment.

SUMMARY

War dialing is a classic attack methodology that seeks to find modems installed within your environment. Over the years, VPN access utilizing the Internet for connections has replaced dial-in telephone lines utilizing modems as the primary remote access solutions of most companies. However, this does not mean that modems have disappeared from modern networks. Modems are still deployed for many reasons, including remote administrative management and manufacturer support for equipment and remote access solutions for areas of the world where high-bandwidth Internet connections are still expensive or not available.

Attackers will utilize publicly available information and social engineering techniques to identify a valid range of phone numbers for an organization before using war dialing software to scan that range for possible targets. The same methodology behind war dialing has been adapted and utilized to form other attacking techniques including port scanning, war driving, and social war dialing. Organizations need to develop and maintain defensive postures against war dialing (even if they officially no longer have modems in their environment), and this should include the reducing or eliminating of modems, the hardening of both the modems and the systems they are connected to, and a system of testing their own environments for rogue modems.

Endnotes

1. Silverthorne S. Feds bust kid hacker, ZDNet, <http://www.infosecnews.org/hypermail/9803/0073.html/>; 1998 [retrieved 28.02.2010].
2. Badham J. WarGames (Movie), Perf. Matthew Broderick, United Artists; 1983.
3. Asimov I. I, Robot, New York: Gnome Press; 1950. Reprinted from New York: Bantam Spectra; 2008.

Penetration "Testing"

INFORMATION IN THIS CHAPTER

- How Penetration Testing Software Works
- Dangers with Penetration Testing Tools
- Future of Penetration Testing Tools
- Defenses against Penetration Testing Software

The practice of penetration testing and the use of specific tools to conduct penetration testing activities are vital parts of vulnerability identification and securing networks. Penetration testing also helps an organization determine how susceptible or resilient to attack it really is. The process of penetration testing involves a great deal of time and dedication to ensure a positive outcome for both the penetration tester and the organization being evaluated. Comparing penetration testing to other real-world types of assessment can help clarify the value of penetration testing.

In 2005, Discovery Channel[A] aired a television series named "It Takes a Thief."[B] This television show was hosted by two former burglars who would identify homes and businesses with weak security controls protecting the valuables stored within. The hosts of the show would obtain permission from home and business owners to demonstrate how easily a burglar could break into the property and walk away with thousands of dollars in valuables. After the burglary was completed, the hosts would explain how they gained access to the property and provide the owners with constructive advice on how to protect themselves from future burglaries. The hosts would also arrange for new security controls to be implemented to help protect the owners from future attacks and then test the controls by trying to break into the property again several weeks later.

"It Takes a Thief" provided value to the home and business owners involved with the TV series, and that value is almost identical to what penetration testers provide

---

[A]http://dsc.discovery.com/
[B]http://dsc.discovery.com/fansites/ittakesathief/ittakesathief.html

businesses today. So how does this tie us into the content of this chapter? How about the tools used to break into the houses and businesses? In many cases, the hosts of the show used readily available tools to circumvent controls. A lock-picking kit can be used by locksmiths to help you out when you're locked out of your home or car, but it can also be used by a thief. A credit card can be used to buy your children ice cream but can also be used to bypass the locking mechanism on a door. This chapter presents a view of "penetration testing" tools and techniques that can be used for both good and immoral purposes.

Just as it took the hosts of "It Takes a Thief" time to perfect their trade, penetration testers and malicious attackers spend many years learning the art of exploitation and the tools used to help them become successful. Some of the concepts and attacks covered in this chapter are very elementary as they apply to securing your organization. Learning more about the tools used by penetration testers and attackers and how they can be used to gain access is a vital part of securing any network. Although, always ensure your defensive strategy is focused more on reducing the likelihood of a threat being realized and not so much on the defense against a particular tool.

HOW PENETRATION TESTING SOFTWARE WORKS

Any good handyman always has a well-equipped tool kit for taking care of repair tasks around the house. While making repairs, we must make sure the appropriate tools are readily available to complete the tasks properly. Having the proper tools allows us to expedite the completion of tasks, which can free up more time for us to spend with our families. Additionally, making sure you have reliable up-to-date tools is important to making sure you maximize your efforts.

As with the handyman and his toolkit, penetration testing software has to be as reliable as possible to make testing networks for vulnerabilities both accurate and efficient. The tools used to perform penetration tests should be field-tested to ensure the reliability of the tools and the safety of the network the tools are being used against.

Another important aspect to consider is the frequency with which tools are updated. Tools in active development and maintenance cycles must stay current to continue detecting the most recent vulnerabilities as well as exploiting them. For this reason, many network security tool developers will provide updates for tools to ensure the tools continue to grow to meet the demands of the security community. Updates to tools not only include feature enhancements and extension to the core components of the tools but also include the libraries required to support them. Additionally, updates to tools may be as simple as deploying new "signatures" for detection purposes.

The groups and individuals who spend time developing security-related assessment tools are dedicated to providing accurate detection and exploitation of vulnerabilities and are usually very skilled at what they do. From simple Ruby or Perl scripts to advanced frameworks, the tools available today for penetration testing and hacking are becoming available to the white hat and black hat communities more rapidly than ever before. Social media, collaboration sites embracing open-source development, and the ability to collaborate freely have made assessment tools significantly easier to develop and distribute than in the past.

Before getting too immersed into the discussion on how penetration testing software works, let's address an important detail regarding who uses the tools and how to determine whether the tools are for penetration testing or hacking. This is a really tricky question and is not always something easy for people to identify. Many of the penetration testers working in the field today refer to themselves as "hackers" even though corporate America has provided them fancy titles like Security Analyst, Vulnerability Researcher, Penetration Tester, and Ethical Hacker.

There is no standard used to classify what is a penetration testing tool used by "penetration testers" and what is a hacking tool used by hackers. The truth of the matter is hackers use "penetration testing tools" and penetration testers use "hacking tools," and the way the tools are used depends on the undertaking of the user. For instance, one popular tool for password attacks against a variety of protocols is THC-Hydra.[C] This tool may be used by both "malicious hackers" and "penetration testers"; however, depending on the purpose of the attack, the tool can be a penetration testing or hacking tool.

A penetration tester may explain his or her use of the tool during a penetration test as "I used Hydra to perform a dictionary attack on the secure shell (SSH) interface of the Cisco router, but no valid credentials were identified. XYZ company should continue using strong passwords that helped make this device secure," whereas a malicious attacker may articulate "I tried to break into my school network, but Hydra did not find any good passwords." What is the real difference between these statements? Nothing except the fact that the penetration tester was using the tool for proactive identification of potential vulnerabilities and the malicious hacker was using the tool for nefarious reasons.

Many people will make the argument that it is bad for penetration testers to make tools public so that not only other security professionals but also attackers with malicious intent will have access to them. However, compare this to going to your local retailer and buying a knife for cooking. Bad guys can buy knives also; is it the knife that is dangerous or how it is intended to be used?

One of the key things that may determine how tools are used is the scope of testing a penetration tester can perform based on Service Level Agreements (SLAs). Testing needs to be accurate and provide value to identifying vulnerabilities, but one disadvantage is that sometimes business contracts and the criticality of systems will limit some of the attacks that can be performed. As a penetration tester, it would be bad business for you to accidently cause a denial of service (DoS) against a critical network asset causing revenue loss for an organization. However, an attacker with malicious intent is not bound by the same rules.

[C]http://freeworld.thc.org/thc-hydra/

EPIC FAIL

Sometimes organizations will request testers to refrain from assessing entire networks because they contain "critical assets." Many times the reason for the exclusion of specific targets is to ensure customers do not experience a degradation of service quality. This is understandable from a business perspective; however, from a testing methodology standpoint, it is a severely flawed practice.

Business rules and SLAs are in place during penetration tests to protect the reliability of service provided to internal and external customers. However, excluding the assessment of resources can provide a false sense of security for organizations that do not ensure penetration tests emulate real-world attacks.

Critical systems should be tested just as any other system to ensure critical operations are not exposed to significant vulnerabilities. If the system is critical, it should have load-balancing capabilities and redundancy implemented to protect against possible outages or degradation. Consider allowing the assessment to be conducted during nonpeak hours to reduce the impact if an unexpected condition occurs. This will be far better than finding out an attacker has taken control of critical systems because of a poor configuration or missing patch that was not identified.

Penetration testers and malicious attackers may use the same tools; in some cases, penetration testers will not be able to use all the functionality of the tools if they reduce the stability of the systems being assessed. If the goal of penetration testing activities is to test for a DoS condition, this limitation may not apply.

DANGERS WITH PENETRATION TESTING TOOLS

Having spent a good amount of time talking about penetration tools and the gray area about what a hacker tool is and is not, let us look at some attacks and how penetration testing tools can be used to maximize the effectiveness and efficiency of an attack. Although several tools will be discussed, it is impossible to cover every tool an attacker may require in one chapter or even an entire book. The tools and scenarios that follow provide an overview to help us understand the potential impact penetration testing tools can have on your organization.

Nessus Vulnerability Scanning

Nessus[D] is a tool that has been used by security professionals for many years. This tool is a vulnerability scanner that allows network security professionals and administrators to audit their networks by scanning ranges of Internet Protocol (IP) addresses and identifying vulnerabilities with a series of *plug-ins*. These plug-ins are written using a language called the *Nessus Attack Scripting Language* (NASL).

NASL plug-ins are a core part of the Nessus platform and are used to identify specific vulnerabilities and flaws in network resources. One of the great features of

---

[D]www.nessus.org/nessus/

Nessus is that anyone can write NASL plug-ins and implement them as part of the scanner. Custom plug-ins can be written to detect vulnerabilities specific to the organization that developed the plug-in. Additionally the plug-ins can be shared with the Nessus development team and may be included in updates to the Nessus platform.

Configuring the initial setup of the Nessus server and client application takes only a few minutes. After setting up the application and determining the scope of the vulnerability scan, the attacker can configure the scanner to scan a single IP address or entire blocks of IP addresses. The time required for a scan to complete depends on how many plug-ins are being used, throughput of the network, scan speed settings, and the number of IP addresses included in the scan.

Once Nessus is configured to scan a network and the scan completes, the vulnerabilities are reported back to the Nessus application. The Nessus application can then present the data gathered back to the user in a variety of helpful formats. In many cases, the Nessus Client application will present information about all the network elements (indicated by their IP addresses) identified during the scans, information gathered from services detected running on the elements, and information about the vulnerabilities that may be associated with the services. This information usually includes detailed information about the vulnerabilities found, including links to Web sites with more detailed information.

Nessus also indicates the severity of vulnerabilities as part of the report details, so administrators and security professionals can identify possible steps to remediate the issues identified. In some cases, Nessus will also present the user with possible remediation steps and general recommendations for fixing identified issues, in addition to links to vulnerability databases that can provide more information on the inner workings of how vulnerabilities can be leveraged.

The system the attacker scanned (in the simulated virtual machine lab environment) is a Windows XP computer with missing security patches. The scan provided many results; however, the vulnerability the attacker appears to be interested in is the MS08-067 Security Bulletin[E] identified in his or her scan report (Figure 3.1).

With the information provided by the Nessus scanner and the reports it generates, it is easy to see how an attacker can use this tool to identify vulnerabilities in network resources. You may also be considering the value this tool can provide for identifying missing patches in your own organization. Once an attacker has used a tool such as Nessus to identify vulnerabilities, he or she will then use the information learned to move on to the exploitation phase of the attack.

NOTE

Scanners such as Nessus are "noisy" when being used with the default settings. Noisy means if Intrusion Detection System (IDS) or Intrusion Prevention System (IPS) is properly configured, it should detect a large amount of network traffic targeting individual or multiple systems with what appears to be suspicious activity. However, attackers may use IDS or IPS evasion technique to elude detection by these systems. Nessus also has the option of using one plug-in at a time to reduce the attack fingerprint and the chances of the malicious activities being detected.

[E]www.microsoft.com/technet/security/Bulletin/MS08-067.mspx

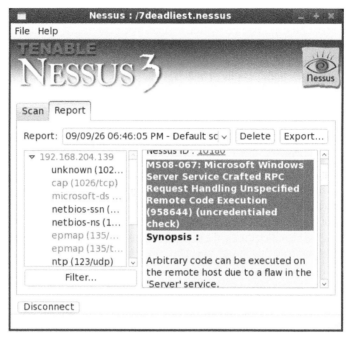

FIGURE 3.1

There are many options for configuration within the Nessus scans, including some options for performing DoS attacks. Refer to Chapter 1, "Denial of Service," for more information on how DoS attacks can cripple networks or even countries. In most cases, the use of DoS attacks is not recommended against production systems unless the specific intent is to verify whether or not a DoS condition is possible for a specific application. These types of tests should be reserved for evaluation during nonpeak hours and ideally with redundant systems in place to take over processing of data should the DoS be successful. Although a penetration tester may have to take all of this into consideration, an attacker may elect to use the DoS plug-ins specifically to cause a disruption or degradation of service. This type of activity can be used to execute a deliberate attack against a primary target or even to distract administrators while the attacker focuses on another target.

Nessus is a great tool for administrators and security professionals to use in their efforts to maintain and assess security within their networks. However, this is an example of a tool attackers can easily use as well. A good part of understanding the best defense is to learn and know the attacks work and how to identify them. It is a good idea to download Nessus to become familiar with the tool and how it can help your organization.

Metasploit Framework

One of the most popular (for good reason) tools out there today is Metasploit.[F] Actually, Metasploit is far more than a tool; it is a framework that encompasses many different capabilities. The Metasploit framework has many different components that make up its functionality. The users, contributors, and developers of Metasploit are very active in its development and maintenance.

The framework can be used for exploit development, penetration testing, creating malicious payloads for client-side attacks, fuzzing, active exploitation, and almost anything you could imagine a penetration tester might need. It can even be used to verify operating system patches applied by network and server administers. A detailed guide for using the Metasploit framework and many of its features can be found at www.offensive-security.com/metasploit-unleashed/. The framework was recently migrated from Perl to Ruby; however, some of the components are implemented with assembler and C.

The framework has many exploits and payloads to choose from to make short work of obtaining administrative access to computers, servers, and network equipment. Exploits are used to leverage flaws or vulnerabilities found in software. Payloads are the code and instructions that allow attackers to interact with compromised systems. This scenario will demonstrate the use of Metasploit to leverage a vulnerability in a computer using the Windows XP operating system and then to use information gleaned from the system to exploit other parts of the network.

Several techniques are used by attackers to discover network resources. Some of the techniques involve mapping the layout of a network, port scanning, and service identification. The focus of this chapter is penetration testing tools and how they can be leveraged for attacks and not a specific tutorial on the use of these techniques for host identification and classification. This first scenario assumes that the target has already been identified and classified by the attacker. The system the attacker has identified is the same system that was previously scanned in the section "Nessus Vulnerability Scanning."

Although Metasploit provides several ways to interact with the framework during attacks in this example, the attacker uses the *msfconsole*. After an attacker has identified and classified a target system, he or she will determine the exploit and payload to use to help him or her achieve his or her goals. In our scenario, the initial goal of the attacker is to compromise a single computer in an effort to learn more information about the network before attacking the Windows Active Directory domain directly.

Figure 3.2 is a screenshot of the attacker preparing his or her exploit and payload to attack a Windows XP operating system that is missing critical patches. The exploit is leveraging the Microsoft Security Bulletin MS08-067[G] vulnerability that affects many of the Microsoft platforms outlined in the referenced link. Metasploit

---

[F]www.metasploit.com/
[G]www.microsoft.com/technet/security/Bulletin/MS08-067.mspx

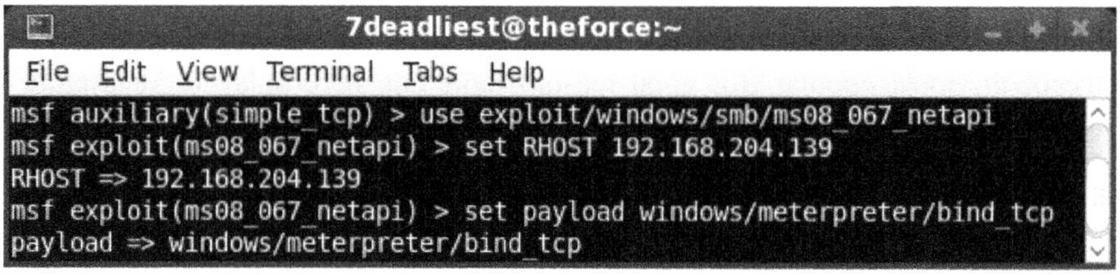

FIGURE 3.2

Exploit Selection

has exploits and payloads to fit many situations including attacks leveraging a large number of Microsoft vulnerabilities.

Once the exploit is successfully executed, the attacker has an opportunity to interact with the operating system and perform a variety of information gathering and other post-exploitation tasks. In this scenario, the attacker decided to use the *meterpreter/bind_tcp* payload to perform some advanced attacks and interact with the compromised computer.

TIP

Meterpreter is a part of the payload that is injected into memory and does not place files on the hard drive. This is achieved by injecting a dynamic link library (DLL) into a process that is already running using a technique called *Remote Library Injection*.[H] The DLL allows attackers to perform tasks that were once complicated in a faster and more efficient manner.

Figure 3.3 demonstrates the attacker executing the previously configured exploit and payload against the Windows XP target. Upon completion of a successful attack, a meterpreter session is started, and the attacker can now take advantage of the functionality meterpreter provides. In our scenario, the attacker uses the *hashdump* command to obtain a copy of the hashed passwords stored on the operating system.

Once the attacker has obtained the password hashes, he or she can crack them offline to obtain the clear-text equivalent and use the passwords obtained to conduct further attacks against the network. Some of the popular tools used for cracking passwords include RainbowCrack,[I] Ophcrack,[J] and John the Ripper.[K] Password attacks and storage are covered in depth in Chapter 1, "Windows Operating System–Password Attacks," of *Seven Deadliest Microsoft Attacks*, another book in the Syngress Seven Deadliest Attacks Series. In many cases, depending on the password complexity, it only takes a few minutes or even a few seconds to crack passwords

---

[H]www.nologin.org/Downloads/Papers/remote-library-injection.pdf
[I]http://project-rainbowcrack.com/
[J]http://ophcrack.sourceforge.net/
[K]www.openwall.com/john/

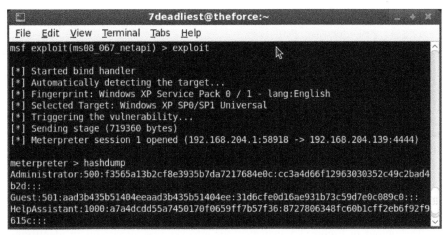

FIGURE 3.3

Password Hashes Obtained

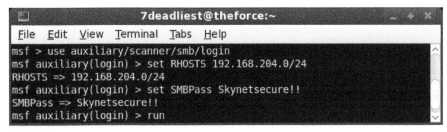

FIGURE 3.4

SMB Login Configurations

using these tools. For those of you who wish to crack the super top-secret password found in Figure 3.3, we will save you the time and let you know the Administrator password will result in a clear-text password of "Skynetsecure!!" (This is one of the passwords used in the VMWare lab environment while working on this book and has no significance outside the lab.)

Now that the attacker has the clear-text equivalent to the hashed password he or she obtained by using the *hashdump* command from within the meterpreter session, he or she can start expanding his or her control ov er the network. Many times administrators will attempt to reduce the complexity of administration of network environments by reusing passwords across multiple systems. With this knowledge, the attacker will now take the credentials he or she obtained from reversing the captured hashes to check if the administrator accounts on other systems within the network are using the same passwords.

In Figure 3.4, the attacker configures one of the Metasploit auxiliary modules to use Server Message Block (SMB) login attempts against multiple systems to reveal if passwords are being reused within the network. The attacker has configured

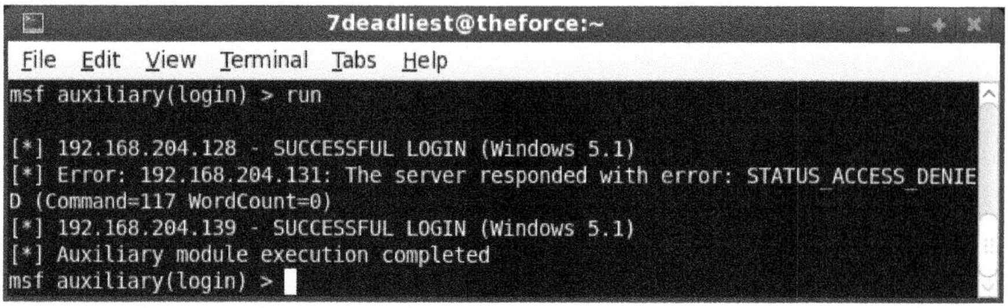

FIGURE 3.5

SMB Login Results

Metasploit to check an entire subnet for computers that accept the username and password using the credentials previously obtained.

The output in Figure 3.5 indicates our attacker was successful in identifying another system using the same password as the one previously compromised. Now the attacker has the ability to take full control of yet another system without having to go through the exploitation phase using a tool similar to Metasploit. This can save the attacker a lot of time while he or she starts taking total control of the systems within the target network.

The VMWare lab environment the attacker was using was limited to five target systems. However, in production networks with hundreds of systems the rewards are often much greater for an attacker. It is not uncommon for penetration testers and attackers to identify many systems reusing passwords, and Metasploit makes easy work of extending an attacker's control of a target network.

Hydra Password Attacks

The last scenario for this chapter explores the types of attacks performed by using Hydra. This tool is one of the best login cracking tools available to penetration testers and attackers due to the number of protocols it supports and the reliability of the results it provides. Currently the tool supports login attacks for over 30 protocols and applications. Some of the protocols supported include SMB, Post Office Protocol 3, Simple Mail Transfer Protocol, telnet, Cisco telnet, Hypertext Transfer Protocol (HTTP), Microsoft Structured Query Language (MSSQL), and MySQL.

This scenario explores the dangers associated with the use of poorly configured management protocols. The attacker has identified what appears to be a Cisco router with telnet and Simple Network Management Protocol (SNMP) enabled. Both of these protocols are used by administrators to remotely administer the device or query performance statistics. The attacker first decides to perform a dictionary attack against the telnet interface but has no success in gaining access to the device.

The attacker decides to focus his or her attacks against the SNMP service running on the device. Attackers can use dictionary attacks against SNMP services just as they can against the telnet interface; however, with SNMP, the password is implemented in the form of a *community string*. This community sting allows administrators to

> **NOTE**
>
> It is common for attackers to use word lists with tools such as Hydra to increase the chances of success while perform password attacks. These word lists may contain many different words that are common in English and other languages.
>
> The "dictionary" part of "dictionary attack" really has two meanings. First, it means a list of words that are compiled to form a dictionary for use in password attacks. Second, a dictionary attack can actually use the entire list of words found in a dictionary. Oxford Dictionary's Web site indicates over 171,000 words[L] in the second edition of their dictionary. This may be a little excessive for dictionary attacks, so it pays to know what the most common words used are.

apply access restrictions to the devices using the SNMP. Typically there are two community strings for management of devices: one of the community strings is usually a *read-only* community string and the other is a *read-write* community string.

Unfortunately, many times the SNMP services on devices are enabled by default and are configured with default community strings. Additionally, if the SNMP service is not enabled, many times administrators will configure SNMP with easily guessable community strings. A few of the most common SNMP community strings seen today are *public*, *private*, *ro*, *rw*, and *internal*. The knowledge of these common configurations allows attackers to use tools such as Hydra to automate the detection of default or easily guessable community strings. Figure 3.6 shows our attacker using Hydra to identify community strings on his or her Cisco router target.

After the scan is completed, the attacker is presented with the results. It appears from the results the attacker was been able to successfully identify two community names "public" and "private." Up to this point, the attacker really did not have any success with gaining access to the network, but because he or she has the SNMP community strings for a Cisco device, he or she may be able to learn more information to perform additional attacks.

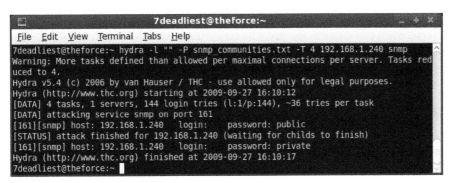

FIGURE 3.6

Hydra SNMP Dictionary Attack

[L]www.askoxford.com/asktheexperts/faq/aboutenglish/numberwords

Since the attacker now has the public and private community strings, he or she may try some advanced attacks that may result in further compromise of the network. The attacker uses the information learned to conduct his or her next attack against the network. By knowing the public community string, he or she is able to query configuration parameters of the device; however, with the private community string, he or she has read or write access to the device.

The attacker uses the knowledge of SNMP, Management Information Base (MIB), and Trivial File Transfer Protocol (TFTP) to transfer the Cisco router configuration file to a remote TFTP server. This is accomplished by the attacker setting up a TFTP server to listen for incoming TFTP write requests and then using the MIB Object Identifiers (OIDs) and the *snmpset* command to instruct the router to transfer its configuration file to the TFTP server. Once the attacker has performed the attack successfully, he or she can use TFTP to retrieve the file transferred to the TFTP server. A detailed explanation on how to use SNMP, MIB, and OIDs for this type of attack can be found on Cisco's support site.[M] Although the Cisco Web site demonstrates the use of this type of functionality with the legitimate user in mind, we can see how an attacker can use it to his or her advantage.

Once the file is retrieved by the attacker, he or she can now review the router configuration file and learn more about the layout of the network, the protocols used, the access lists implemented, and possibly the password of the router. If the passwords configured for the device are stored in clear text, then the attacker may be able to use this password to gain access to network components or cause a DoS by reconfiguring the router to drop all legitimate traffic.

WARNING

In some cases, the Cisco passwords may be encrypted using the *service password-encryption* command. This will result in the encryption of the passwords using a weak Cisco "Type 7" proprietary encryption algorithm that can be reversed to its clear-text equivalent by using publicly available tools such as Cain and Abel.[N]

Although this scenario focused a lot on the exploitation of a router by manipulating SNMP, the tool that made this all possible was Hydra. There are many other types of attacks an attacker can perform against many protocols using this powerful tool.

FUTURE OF PENETRATION TESTING TOOLS

Many of the tools attackers and penetration testers have today are the work of years and years of labor by skilled tool developers. As the population of people who are interested in network security grows, the interest and support in tool and exploit

---

[M]www.cisco.com/en/US/tech/tk648/tk362/technologies_tech_note09186a008009463e.shtml
[N]www.oxid.it/cain.html

Table 3.1 Top 10 penetration testing tools[o]	
Top 10 tools – sectools.org	
Nessus	Hping2
Wireshark	Kismet
Snort	Tcpdump
Netcat	Cain and Abel
Metasploit Framework	John the Ripper

development grows. The focus on frameworks has allowed many people to contribute to larger projects such as Metasploit. With the ease of use of these frameworks, we find that more people are willing to contribute to the development of the framework or projects that support the framework.

The number of tools available today is staggering. Tools are developed to support the assessment of almost every major protocol or application deployed on a wide variety of network types. Even those who work in the security field or those who are conducting malicious attacks on a regular basis cannot keep up with the abundance of tools available. However, there are tools used so often that they deserve to be mentioned. A comprehensive list of the top 100 tools in use can be found at http://sectools.org/. The list was the result of an extensive survey conducted in 2006 by *Fyodor* (Gordon Lyon[p]) of Insecure.org, and many of the tools listed are still very relevant today and will be for years to come. The top 10 tools from the list are included in Table 3.1.

Although these have been identified as the top 10 tools from the survey, many other tools on the survey are used by penetration testers and attackers. It depends on the goal of the hack to determine what tools will be used to help achieve the desired results.

DEFENSES AGAINST PENETRATION TESTING SOFTWARE

So, what can we do about protecting ourselves from the dangers associated with penetration testing tools? It appears we are caught in the cross fire of good versus evil, and both sides have quite an arsenal of weapons to choose from. How do we protect ourselves against tools we are supposed to be using to evaluate our own security? In some cases, the answers to these questions will be very clear, but in other cases, it may take a little more creativity to arrive at a workable solution.

---

[o]http://sectools.org/
[p] http://insecure.org/fyodor/

Password Complexity, Lockouts, and Logging

One of the tools discussed during this chapter was THC-Hydra. The tool provides malicious attackers, auditors, network administrators, and penetration testers with an automated method of testing network services for weak passwords. Administrators have a few things they can do to prevent or reduce the success of attacks using this and other similar tools.

First and foremost, do not use weak passwords. One of the easiest ways to compromise networks is by identifying services with weak or no passwords in place. Administrators must ensure complex passwords are being implemented to help prevent the success of attack using THC-Hydra and other logon cracking tools. Complex passwords should have certain attributes that qualify them as being strong.

Passwords should be at least 8 characters long. The larger the password the better, as it will require more computations and larger dictionaries for computers to process before finding the proper password. In time any password is crackable; it is the job of the administrator to ensure passwords are strong enough to defeat logon crackers and working with a longer password helps make it more challenging.

To offset the likelihood of passwords being cracked, administrators should also enforce the use of complex passwords. Complex passwords are usually long and use more of the key space found on keyboards. This means user should not only use uppercase and lowercase characters but also use numbers and symbols. Numbers and symbols can also be used to replace traditional letters found on the keyboard. As an example, the password "Skynetsecure!!" is fairly strong to begin with due to its complexity and length; however, additional modifications to the passwords can make it even more secure. By applying more of the key space, we can modify this passwords to be "$kyn3ts3(uR3!!," which is certainly more complex than the previous example.

Implementing lockout policies is also a very important part of reducing the attack surface of logon cracking attacks. Lockout policies apply rules of how the system will react in the event multiple logon attempts fail. For instance, if a policy dictates that a user account will be locked out for 30 min after 3 logon attempts fail, this will limit the number of attempts an attacker can make in a given day. Modifying the policy to lock out the account for 60 min will reduce the likelihood of success even further.

Something to consider about usability and overhead associated with long, complex passwords and lockout thresholds is the overhead it may cause for support functions within the organization. Help-desk calls may increase causing additional overhead due to the length and complexity of the passwords and the human ability to properly enter their password when required. Careful consideration and research should be done before changing your network's password policies. It is also recommended to notify employees that a password policy change may be coming in the future, so they have time to mentally prepare for the change and can adopt the change with little frustration.

Logging also plays an important role for defending against penetration testing or hacking tools and suspicious network activity. Configuring logging and most importantly notification of critical errors can provide advanced warning about active and pending attacks against the organization. Implementing lockout policies is important, but being able to identify accounts being locked out or multiple failed logon attempts may tip off administrators that something malicious may be taking place.

Finally, don't just log it, review it. There is no sense in logging critical security events if no one is going to review or be notified of the events. Real-time notification should be considered, especially when you have a situation where an attacker is attempting to access network resources. It is not a good idea to wait for the help-desk group to notify you of something suspicious because of an increase in call volume due to user's accounts needing to be unlocked. Get the information straight from the source and in real time by being notified of account lockouts automatically.

Endpoint Protection

Implementing standard virus and malware protection on the desktop can help identify malicious activity as well. Many antivirus software products can detect common tools and classify them as hacking tools. Although implementing antivirus protection should not be a standalone solution, it may help detect tools being used if an attacker is being sloppy with his or her work.

Once again, ensure notification of virus, malware, and hacking tools is being logged to a centralized server, and notifications are sent to administrators where possible. Many times the classification of an item being detected as a hack tool should raise specific concerns. This notification can mean an attacker has already gained access to a system and is uploading malicious tools, or a curious employee is installing malicious tools indicating a possible insider threat.

Egress Filtering and Proxies

Just as firewalls have rules to allow or deny access to resources within a demilitarized zone and between internal networks based on the type of network traffic, egress filtering addresses the data trying to leave your network. Many organizations focus too much attention on protecting the network from attacks sourcing from external threats, and not enough attention is focused on what is happening within the network.

Properly implemented egress filtering can help administrators detect malicious or suspicious traffic as it attempts to leave the network. Egress filtering also provides some flexibility while an organization is trying to reduce the effects of malware. Several vendors offer solutions to implement application layer proxies and content filters to help prevent malicious outbound connections from within the trusted network. Some of the concepts of egress filtering are covered in the National Institute of Standards and Technologies (NIST) special publications 800-61[Q] and 800-83.[R]

[Q]http://csrc.nist.gov/publications/nistpubs/800-61/sp800-61.pdf
[R]http://csrc.nist.gov/publications/nistpubs/800-83/SP800-83.pdf

One of the most popular implementations of outbound proxies is its use for content filtering by forcing all HTTP traffic through a HTTP or a HTTPS proxy. This allows security administrators to keep better control of the flow of traffic in and out of the organization and an opportunity to identify malicious activity. The use of proxies also allows organizations to minimize the spread of malicious code as a result of viruses and malware.

Intrusion Detection and Prevention

Intrusion detection and prevention implementations can also help detect malicious activity as it occurs within a network. Many vendors provide good solutions for detecting threats, and most have the ability to immediately report suspicious activity or attack signatures to network administrators and security personnel.

As an example, consider the possibility an attacker is currently performing a dictionary attack against the telnet interface on the router your company uses to connect to the Internet. This interface was left in place so the maintenance company contracted to perform routine maintenance and upgrades can have access when they need to troubleshoot problems. A properly placed and configured IDS or IPS should be able to trigger an alert when it notices hundreds of authentication attempts per minute are being made to the telnet interface from single or multiple IP addresses.

IDS and IPS platforms can also detect malicious network activity based on variances in what "normal" network traffic for your network looks like. This type of detection is referred to as an "anomaly"-based IDS or IPS. The advantage of using an IDS or IPS that detects suspicious traffic is that the system has an established baseline for how your network normally operates and can compare traffic patterns to the baseline. Should suspicious network traffic be identified, administrators can be notified so further investigation can be conducted.

Logical Access Controls

The final defensive measure covered in this chapter is the use of logical access controls to restrict access to services based on criteria set by administrators. The concept of logical access controls is nothing new, but the impact they can have on security if implemented properly can be profound. An easy-to-understand example of logical access controls is implementing access control lists to limit access to protocols used for remote administration.

Remote administration is a fact of life for many large organizations. Due to the geographical separation of administrators from the systems they manage, many times administrative functions occur from remote subnets, cities, or even countries. Because of the dynamic nature of networking and administration, many times administrators will implement remote administration interfaces without regard to who will actually have access to them.

One of the dangers associated to implementing administrative interfaces without proper controls in place is that anyone who can access the interface can attempt to authenticate and possibly gain access to administrative functions. Logical access controls can help bridge this security gap.

For example, administrators can implement logical access controls that only allow connection to administrative interfaces from IP addresses or management subnets that are predefined by the administrators. This allows legitimate administrators to connect to the management interfaces and conduct their business but denies access to those connections that are not defined as part of the logical access control rules.

Of course, there is always a caveat to what we think is a great plan. If one of the systems we defined as valid system to conduct administrative tasks with is compromised, an attacker will be able to circumvent the logical access controls altogether. This is why it is important to consider implementing controls in addition to logical access controls, such as the use of certificates for authentication.

SUMMARY

As discussed in the introduction, the use of penetration testing tools is a vital part of the assessment of networks. The content of this chapter provided some insight into how penetration tools can benefit both the penetration tester and the malicious hacker in the goal of identifying and exploiting vulnerabilities.

Some of the scenarios presented in the chapter also explained how common penetration testing and hacking tools work. The scenarios also displayed how such tools can have a significant impact on the security of those organizations that fail to implement proper security controls.

The penetration testing tools we talked about in this chapter are just the tip of the iceberg. Just like an iceberg, there is usually a lot more under the surface you may not readily see at first. Many more great tools exist in the security community, but in many cases, you do not discover them until you have had some time to explore and encounter situations where special tools are required.

Finally, some of the defensive techniques discussed can help reduce your exploitable footprint. It is likely many other defensive measures will need to be considered to mitigate threats, but the options discussed in this chapter should provide some sound advice to get you started.

Protocol Tunneling

INFORMATION IN THIS CHAPTER

- How Protocol Tunneling Works
- Dangers of Protocol Tunneling
- Defending against Protocol Tunneling
- The Future of Protocol Tunneling

You're at work and bored as usual. You decide to take some time off from monitoring network security alerts to download some music. You hop on the Internet, download a peer-to-peer (P2P) file-sharing program, and install it on your company laptop. Nice. Now you're ready to download.

Your first few searches don't seem to work, and soon you've figured out why. At the bottom of the window is a little icon that indicates that the file-sharing program has detected a firewall. You are being blocked by your company's Internet policies. The software needs port 45114 open, but it is closed. A little experimentation reveals that the company is blocking traffic on *most* ports. It's frustrating; it is like they *don't* want you downloading. Worse, the thought occurs to you that they might even monitor your Internet use.

Fortunately, you know about *protocol tunneling*. After a few minutes you've created an encrypted connection between your laptop and your home computer. Now all the P2P traffic goes through the tunnel to your computer, and then out to the Internet. Others on the P2P network can connect to your home computer and their traffic is encrypted and sent to your work laptop. Soon you are listening to music and silently laughing at the information technology (IT) department's feeble attempts to block you. If you've configured everything "correctly," others can download files from your hard drive, just as you can from theirs. This might include your music files, your tax return, your company's host lists, or the information on the latest bid your company is planning to submit.

It now appears that a defense contractor in Bethesda, Maryland, had just such a file-sharing program installed on one of their machines. The machine also contained sensitive data: in this case, blueprints for Marine One, the helicopter that transports the President of the United States. File-sharing programs are all about *sharing*, and the blueprints and other information now appear to have been downloaded to a site in Iran, according to officials at Tiversa, Inc., a company that monitors P2P networks for sensitive data.[A] This was not a unique event.[B]

This particular incident may not have been a protocol-tunneling incident *per se*, but it does illustrate the risks. Protocol tunneling can allow employees to inadvertently subvert your company's security policies. Worse, it can allow insiders or attackers to explicitly subvert your security policies to exfiltrate data, or establish a command and control channel for further hacking.

Unlike most of the other subjects in this text, there is nothing inherently dangerous about protocol tunneling. Sometimes it is a good thing, and sometimes it is essential for maintaining security. If your company requires you to use a virtual private network (VPN) to connect, they are requiring you to use protocol tunneling. Protocol tunneling is an essential enabling technology, but it can enable both good and bad Internet behavior.

EPIC FAIL

Of course, you're careful about file-sharing software and would never inadvertently share your tax return, old love letters, or your *Star Trek* fan script. You have nothing to worry about, right?

Maybe. But others may have your information, too, and might not be so careful. On July 9, 2008, The Washington Post reported on an investment firm employee who decided to install and run the LimeWire[C] file-sharing program. When he or she did this, he or she inadvertently shared out his or her firm's files to the world. This information included names, social security numbers, and dates of birth for about 2,000 of the firm's clients. Among these clients was Supreme Court Justice Stephen Breyer.[D]

HOW PROTOCOL TUNNELING WORKS

Simply put, protocol tunneling (or just *tunneling*) is using one communication protocol, say the Hypertext Transfer Protocol (HTTP) that allows the Web to function, to transmit data in another protocol, say for a P2P network.

Protocol tunneling relies on the simple fact that a communications medium that allows you to transmit information of *some* kind can be exploited to transmit *any* kind of information (though perhaps at a greatly reduced rate).

[A] www.wpxi.com/news/19377076/detail.html

[B] For another example of data exfiltration using P2P network software, see the article "Army Special Forces Document Leaked On P2P Network," in SC Magazine. At the time of writing, this was available online from www.scmagazineus.com/Army-Special-Forces-document-leaked-on-P2P-network/article/151309/.

[C] www.limewire.com/

[D] www.washingtonpost.com/wp-dyn/content/article/2008/07/08/AR2008070802997.html

We can illustrate this with the following example. Suppose you are offered money for sensitive information from your company. Security is tight, and no electronic media can leave the site, but you do have access to a customer-facing support site set up by your company to answer customer support questions. Perfect! You wait for a customer to post a complicated question about configuration. Your reply includes a series of screenshots that show how to do the configuration. The site is monitored, but there is nothing wrong with your message. In fact, going the extra mile with the screenshots earns you an "attaboy" from your supervisor. Encoded within the screenshots is the sensitive data. You've just used the Internet, a blog, and digital *steganography*, concealment of a secret message in such a way that the existence of the secret message is itself hidden, to exfiltrate data. Software to do this encoding is readily available and easy to use.[E]

In general, protocol tunneling of arbitrary data through a firewall requires just three elements:

- Access to a computer inside the firewall.
- Access to a computer outside the firewall.
- A communication channel that connects the two.

If an employee or an attacker has these three items, protocol tunneling can be used to transmit data and bypass a firewall.

NOTE

Are you running Microsoft Windows Vista? It has protocol tunneling built in.

The Internet Protocol (IP) controls how data is transferred on the Internet. At present, most Internet traffic uses the IPv4 version of this protocol. IPv6 is the designated successor to IPv4, but adoption is progressing slowly because of legacy equipment and software.

If you want to use IPv6, but are sitting behind an IPv4 router, what are you to do? Well, why not tunnel IPv6 over IPv4? That's precisely what the Teredo software that is part of Windows Vista does. This software is enabled by default.

Is this a problem? Unless your network security devices and software are Teredo-aware, this can effectively bypass them, creating a security risk. James Hoagland of Symantec wrote a paper on just this subject in 2006: "The Teredo Protocol: Tunneling Past Network Security and Other Security Implications."[F]

Teredo can be disabled as follows. Open the Windows **Control Panel** and click on **System and Maintenance**. Click on **Device Manager**. In the device manager, select **Show Hidden Devices** from the **View** menu. Now expand the **Network Adapters** node in the device list. You should see *Teredo Tunneling Pseudo Interface* in the list. Right-click this entry and select **Disable**. Also disable the *6to4 Adapter* in the list.

It is probably a good idea to restart the computer after this change.

[E]BitCrypt is one open-source steganographic tool for hiding information in images. The information is first encrypted and then the encrypted message is hidden in an image. At the time of writing, BitCrypt is available for free from http://bitcrypt.moshe-szweizer.com/.

[F]The paper is available from Symantec's Web site: www.symantec.com/.

The Great Firewall

China's Golden Shield project, widely known to the rest of the world as the Great Firewall of China, is an attempt to control access to the Internet by various methods, including blocking certain Internet addresses, blocking or redirecting specific hosts and domains, URL filtering, and even packet filtering.[G] Despite these efforts, there are still unblocked communications channels (or nothing would get through). This has spawned a cottage industry of tools for bypassing the Great Firewall. Some of these include the following.

- The Gollum "browser" uses advanced Web technology to allow access to the English language Wikipedia from within China.[H]
- Freegate and UltraSurf are anti-censorship tools that use P2P-like protocol tunnel network to transmit data.[I]

Setting Up a Channel with SSH

One of the most common protocol tunnels to establish is a secure shell (SSH) tunnel. This uses the SSH tool to create an encrypted tunnel between two computers. The channel encrypts and decrypts any data sent, and any information may be sent through the channel. This allows setting up secure versions of otherwise insecure connections, such as mail, File Transfer Protocol, and remote desktop. It can also be used to bypass a firewall.

Suppose you've discovered that you can't access some service from work (bittorrent, instant messaging, or perhaps your favorite "graphics" site). Or perhaps you don't like having your Internet browsing monitored. Sure, you spend most of your time at work on social networking sites arguing about whether Kirk or Picard was the best captain of the Enterprise, but that's not your boss' business, now is it? You decide to use SSH to create a secure tunnel, bypass the company firewall and packet monitoring system, and cloak your traffic.

Recall what is needed for protocol tunneling. You have access to your machine at work (inside the firewall), but you need access to a machine outside the firewall. There are a few possibilities.

- You can get an SSH account on an SSH provider. There are many Internet service providers (ISPs) that offer SSH accounts, at varying prices. A quick visit to Google at the time of writing turned up several sites with plans under $10 per month.[J]

[G]On May 20, 2008, the U.S. Senate Judiciary Committee held a hearing titled "Global Internet Freedom: Corporate Responsibility and the Rule of Law" that discusses both Internet censorship and the technologies that are used to bypass it. At the time of writing the webcast and transcripts are available from http://judiciary.senate.gov/. In particular, Dr. Shiyu Zhou discussed China's Golden Shield project and the role of U.S. companies operating in China.
[H]http://gollum.easycp.de/en/
[I]Freegate: www.dit-inc.us/freegate/. UltraSurf: www.ultrareach.com/.
[J]The site www.red-pill.eu/freeunix.shtml lists (at the time of writing) several free shell providers, including http://freeshell.org/ and www.grex.org/.

- You might have an SSH-enabled account already. If you are a student, or if you have an alumnus account at a college, you may have an account on the school's machines.
- You might have an always-on Internet connection at home. If so, great! You completely control a machine outside the firewall. The trick is getting to it. If your ISP gives you a different IP address every time you connect, you can use a dynamic domain name system (DNS) service to assign your machine an Internet accessible name.[K]

Let's assume you want to create a tunnel for browsing the Web. Figure 4.1 illustrates the usual way of connecting to a Web site. Your machine makes a connection through the company firewall to port 80 (or port 443 for HTTPS) on the remote machine. Because your traffic passes "in the clear" through the firewall, your company IT department can monitor, or restrict, your Internet use.

Let's suppose your home machine is accessible as home.dynamic.example. Even better, you can get to it from work via HTTP and SSH, both of which are commonly allowed through firewalls. The desired situation is illustrated in Figure 4.2. Now only encrypted SSH traffic passes through the company firewall, to your home machine's SSH port, port 22. Your home machine acts as a *proxy*, and makes a connection on your behalf with the remote machine, on port 80. Traffic again passes in both directions, but only "in the clear" between your home machine and the remote machine. Your company IT department sees only the encrypted traffic.

You will pay a penalty for this in terms of bandwidth. First, your home machine probably doesn't have the same bandwidth as your company machine or the remote machine, so it slows down the traffic. You can possibly overcome this by leasing an SSH account from an ISP. Second, there is overhead associated with encrypting and decrypting the traffic on your work machine and your home machine, though this

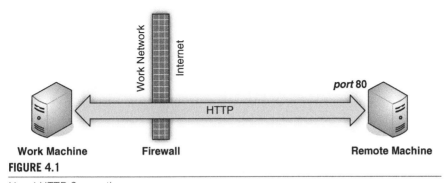

Work Machine   **Firewall**   **Remote Machine**

FIGURE 4.1

Usual HTTP Connection

[K]Again, a quick trip to Google reveals several free dynamic DNS services. DHIS (www.dhis.org/) and DynDNS (www.dyndns.com/) both provide free dynamic DNS services.

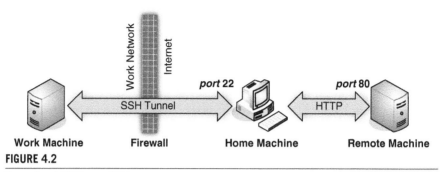

FIGURE 4.2

Tunneling HTTP over SSH

is small. Finally, your outgoing traffic must include both the SSH protocol traffic and your tunneled HTTP traffic. Overall, however, you will probably find this quite acceptable.

Configuring SSH

Now that you've planned your tunnel, your next step is to download and install SSH software on both your work machine and your home machine. You have choices. There are both commercial[L] and open-source implementations.[M] PuTTY[N] is a SSH client commonly used on Windows machines. It is also common to install OpenSSH under Cygwin,[O] a UNIX-like environment for Windows.

Okay, you've downloaded and installed the OpenSSH server on your home machine. Sadly, you are not able to install software on your work machine. No problem. You only need to run the client, and you can probably run it as a regular user. Let's assume your work machine is a Windows machine, and you plan to use PuTTY on it. You can just download the putty.exe executable, and run it locally.

Next, you need to set up a tunnel. Modern SSH clients support the SOCKS[P] protocol, an Internet proxy protocol. All you really need to know is that the SSH client software on your machine is going to send your Web requests to your home machine, which will forward them on to the correct host, just as you want.

Double-click the **putty.exe** you downloaded earlier to start PuTTY. The PuTTY configuration dialog will open. Enter the remote host name in **Host Name** (Figure 4.3). If you have changed the port used by SSH (more on that in a bit), then you should set the correct port here; otherwise leave it at **22**, which is the default for SSH. Do not click **Open** yet!

Expand **SSH** on the left, and then select **Tunnels**. You need to choose a port on your local machine that is not otherwise being used. Values above 10,000 are a fairly safe bet. Let's say you choose 10808. Enter the port number and select **Dynamic**

[L]See SSH Communications Security Crporation, http://ssh.com/.
[M]See OpenSSH, http://openssh.com/.
[N]http://chiark.greenend.org.uk/~sgtatham/putty/.
[O]www.cygwin.com/.
[P]http://tools.ietf.org/html/rfc1928

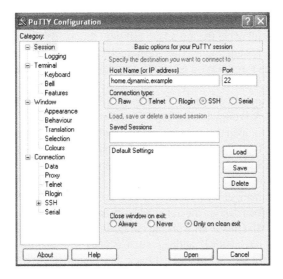

FIGURE 4.3

PuTTY Configuration Dialog

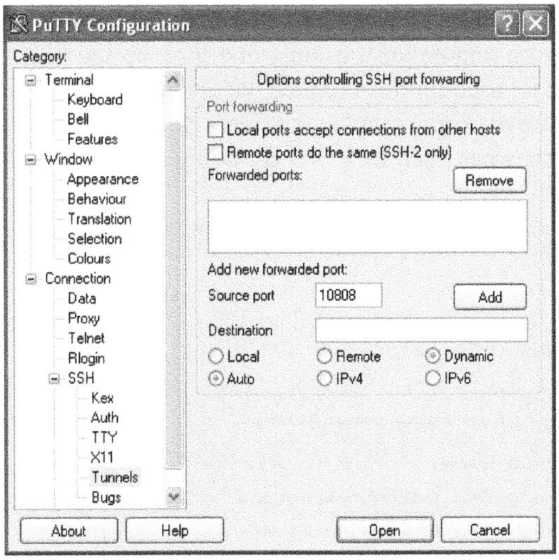

FIGURE 4.4

Tunnel Configured in PuTTY

in the radio buttons. Leave the **Destination** field empty, and click **Add**. The text *D10808* will appear in the list of tunnels (Figure 4.4).

Now you are ready to connect to the remote machine that will do the proxying. Switch back to **Session** at the top left of the dialog, verify the host name, and click **Open**. Log in to your home computer. You've established the tunnel.

Configuring the Browser

Having the tunnel and using the tunnel are different things. By default the software on your work computer is not going to use the tunnel; you need to tell it to use it. This section will discuss the Firefox browser, as it is available on many different platforms.

You need to tell Firefox to use port 10808 as a SOCKS v5 proxy. This is considerably easier than it sounds. From the **Tools** menu select **Options**. The **Options** dialog will appear. Select **Advanced** at the top of the dialog (Figure 4.5).

Click **Settings** to open the network settings dialog. This is where you will add the information about the proxy. Select **manual proxy configuration** and enter **localhost** as the **SOCKS Host** and **10808** as the port and click **OK** (Figure 4.6).

Now you can browse the Web. Firefox will transmit Web requests to port 10808, where SSH will intercept them, encrypt them, and forward them to your home machine. Your home machine will then decrypt the traffic and forward the request on to the correct host.

You can verify that this is all working correctly. There are several services on the Internet that report back your IP address, such as whatismyipaddress.com. Point your browser to one of these; you should get back the IP address of your *home* machine. If you do, everything is working correctly.

Tunneling DNS

There is one minor item of importance. You don't want your boss to see your Internet traffic, and now it is encrypted: so far, so good. However, when your work computer needs to connect to a remote host, it must first look up the host name to get an IP address. The protocol used for this is called the *domain name service*, or DNS. Right now every DNS query is being sent "in the clear," so everyone can see where you are browsing, even if they can't see what you are doing.

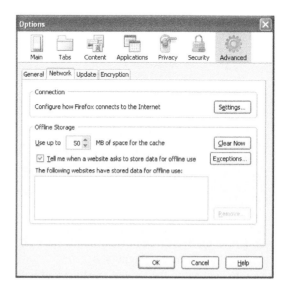

FIGURE 4.5

Firefox Advanced Options

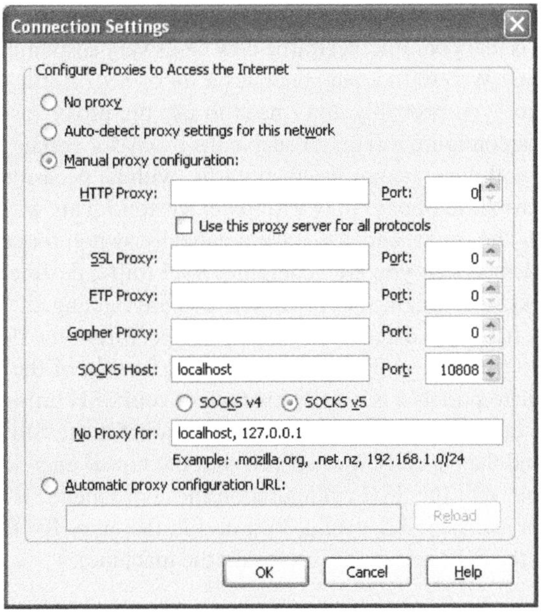

FIGURE 4.6

Configuring a Proxy Server in Firefox

Don't worry, you can tunnel the DNS Protocol, too, and it is easy. In the **location bar** of Firefox enter the text **about:config** and hit Enter. You'll get a scary warning about voiding your warranty, but keep in mind that Firefox comes with *no* warranty, so click the button to continue.

This page lists many different configuration options that are supported by the browser. We only want to change one: **network.proxy.socks_remote_dns**. Find this option and double-click it. The setting should change to **true**. This tells Firefox to send DNS queries to the proxy, so they get encrypted and sent over the SSH tunnel along with all other traffic.

TIP

DNS is itself a protocol; why can't we tunnel our traffic over DNS? That's precisely what OzymanDNS, written by Dan Kaminsky, does.[Q]

In hotels, airports, and other places you may encounter unencrypted public wireless Internet (WiFi). These services typically block your connection to remote hosts unless you pay a fee, but also often allow DNS queries to succeed. By tunneling your traffic over DNS, you can bypass these restrictions. The process to do this is well documented on the Web.[R]

[Q]www.doxpara.com/
[R]www.dnstunnel.de/

Potential Problems

The first problem is that your Internet traffic now looks very suspicious. Your machine never generates any Web traffic, but generates a lot of SSH traffic destined for just one host. In reality, you probably don't need to use the proxy for certain kinds of browsing. You can configure Firefox to enable the proxy for certain sites, but not for others. Now you will generate normal Web traffic, with an occasional SSH connection. To do this, install the FoxyProxy Firefox extension.[S] This will make it easy to enable and disable the proxy, and also to automatically switch for certain URLs.

Another problem is that you are generating SSH traffic destined for your home machine. The folks in IT might start to suspect you are running an SSH tunnel. One way to make this harder to detect is to change the port from the default 22 to 443. Port 443 is the port used by HTTPS, the encrypted version of the HTTP protocol. Because the traffic to port 443 is usually encrypted, your SSH traffic will look much more normal. To do this, you need to modify the port for the SSH server on your home machine, and then specify it when you start the tunnel on your work machine. To change the port, edit the SSH configuration file. For OpenSSH on Linux this is typically found in /etc/ssh/sshd_config. Edit or add the entry for **Port** and set it to **443**. Then restart the SSH server (or just restart the machine).

Corkscrew and SSH over HTTPS

Suppose that your company has realized that someone, possibly you, may exploit SSH to create covert tunnels. They've proactively shut down port 22, and perhaps even installed software to detect SSH. All traffic to the outside world now goes through a proxy server, so you cannot open an arbitrary port. What are you going to do now?

Why not tunnel SSH through the proxy? After all, the proxy exists to let you get to the outside. If it all sounds too complicated, then good news: there are freely available tools to help you set this up. Corkscrew[T] and Proxytunnel[U] both focus on creating an HTTPS tunnel to allow SSH through a proxy server.

SSH over HTTP

If you can use HTTP to transmit hockey scores, wedding photos, e-mail attachments, PDF documents, and Joe Satriani's "It's So Good," then why not SSH? If you can create an SSH tunnel over HTTP, then you can go ahead and create other tunnels over SSH just as before. Even HTTP. Yes, you are going to pay a price in bandwidth, but computers and corporate networks are fast, and getting faster all the time.

It may seem a bit surreal to tunnel HTTP over SSH that is in turn tunneled over HTTP, but that is just what the httptunnel[V] tool is for. You run an httptunnel server on your home machine and an httptunnel client on your work machine.

[S]Firefox extensions can be found at https://addons.mozilla.org/en-US/firefox/.
[T]www.agroman.net/corkscrew/
[U]http://proxytunnel.sourceforge.net/
[V]www.nocrew.org/software/httptunnel.html

Automation

By now you are probably starting to complain about the dizzying technical details. "SSH? HTTPS? Acronyms? Aw...can't someone *else* do all this?" Yes, of course they can. There are turn key solutions to this problem, so let's have a look at some of them.

The Onion Router (Tor)[W] is an open-source implementation of "onion routing," in which several layers of encryption are added to messages. As the messages are passed along the network, each layer of encryption is removed to determine where to send the message next, until it emerges "in the clear" at an endpoint. The primary purpose of Tor is anonymity.

On the subject of anonymity, the Swedish company Relakks runs proxy servers that allow you to tunnel your Web and other Internet traffic anonymously.[X]

Recall httptunnel? If you visited the Web page and read some of the documentation, you might be wondering if someone can't make things simpler. Sure they can. There is a commercial HTTP tunnel client called, interestingly enough, *HTTP-TunnelClient*.[Y]

DANGERS OF PROTOCOL TUNNELING

Protocol tunneling can explicitly bypass security restrictions. In that sense it poses a serious challenge to network security. Further, when coupled with encryption techniques like steganography it becomes nearly impossible to eliminate. The primary dangers posed by protocol tunneling are data exfiltration, hijacking, and enabling direct attacks.

WARNING

"Deep packet inspection," where security devices and software inspect the packets to determine what their payload really is, can detect many common forms of protocol tunneling. Of course, it is still possible to "leak" information out. *Steganography* is the practice of transmitting information in such a way that only the sender and recipient know that there was a transmission at all. Typically the hidden message is embedded in another, typical and unremarkable, message.

It is possible to use steganography to tunnel a protocol over otherwise typical transmissions. One can queue up the data to transmit, wait for outgoing messages, and transmit the tunneled traffic over this otherwise normal traffic. Deep packet inspection will determine this to be expected traffic.[Z]

You should be aware of protocol steganography, as it represents a serious threat for data exfiltration that is not adequately addressed by current technologies.

[W]www.torproject.org/
[X]www.relakks.com/
[Y]www.http-tunnelclient.com/
[Z]This approach is explored in the paper "Syntax and Semantics-Preserving Application-Layer Protocol Steganography," by Norka Lucena, James Pease, Payman Yadollahpour, and Steve Chapin, in *Lecture Notes in Computer Science*, volume 3200/2005, Springer, Berlin, 2005.

Data exfiltration is the most obvious malicious application of protocol tunneling. An insider can use protocol tunneling to transmit confidential information outside the company. A tunnel, once configured and established, can serve as a back door, or *reverse-connect proxy*, allowing subsequent intrusion.

Creating a tunnel entails other risks as well, even if the intent of the tunnel is not malicious. The tunnel can be hijacked, allowing an intruder to compromise security. In the incident described at the beginning of this chapter, the P2P protocol was exploited to gain unauthorized access to confidential information. Older versions of the SSH protocol are subject to hijacking by a kind of man-in-the-middle attack (the subject of Chapter 6, "Man-in-the-Middle") called SSH injection. Nearly all protocols used on the Internet allow bidirectional data transfer; if people can use the tunnel to get out, others may use it to get in.

Finally, a tunnel may be created simply to enable other malicious technologies. Chapter 1, "Denial of Service," explains how networks of compromised machines ("botnets") can be managed using Internet relay chat (IRC), a simple communications protocol. Tunneling IRC over another protocol makes it more difficult to detect these botnets.

Every communications channel can be exploited to create a tunnel. Even one of the simplest Internet protocols, the ICMP echo/reply, also known as *ping*, can be exploited to create a tunnel.[AA] Many Windows machines set their clocks using a protocol known as Network Time Protocol (NTP). A single NTP packet contains four 64-bit timestamp fields, or 32 bytes total. Even though 32 bytes per packet is not a lot of bandwidth, if the message to be sent is small or suitably compressed an NTP tunnel may be sufficient.

DEFENDING AGAINST PROTOCOL TUNNELING

Employees may create protocol tunnels to overcome company network policies, with no malicious intent in mind. However, when the tunnels created bypass the company firewall and network restrictions, they effectively negate a significant part of the network security plan. Whether a tunnel is created explicitly for data exfiltration, or just to enable an Internet radio station, the possibility of an intruder using the tunnel for malicious purposes exists.

As long as you allow access to a communications channel to the outside world, protocol tunneling will be possible. Defenses against this attack therefore tend to fall into one of two categories:

- taking actions to make protocol tunneling harder or less efficient, or
- detecting protocol tunnels.

[AA]See Ping Tunnel, www.cs.uit.no/~daniels/PingTunnel/.

Preventing Protocol Tunneling

If you decide you must make every effort to guard against protocol tunneling, the first step is to close down every unnecessary port (a good idea, anyway). This restricts the channels available to create tunnels. As we have seen, this does not make protocol tunneling impossible, but it does make it harder and may make it easier to detect.

Another strategy is to limit the allowable payload. For example, ICMP tunneling can be overcome by restricting the payload of the packets. If bandwidth is not an issue, however, any allowable variation in payload can be exploited.

An application-level gateway (ALG) can be used to augment your firewall and provide application-level filtering and control of traffic. ALGs understand a variety of protocols, from bittorrent to instant messaging, and can perform *deep packet inspection*, where packets are scanned to determine their purpose and information content. Because of this, an ALG can act as a kind of proxy for the application level traffic. There are a variety of ALG solutions on the market, with a wide range of functionality.[BB]

Open-source solutions exist, as well. Squid is a caching proxy server that also supports content filtering via access control lists (ACL).[CC] Dante is an implementation of the SOCKS protocol that allows for logging, bandwidth control to limit access to nonwork sites, and for implementing quality-of-service (QoS) restrictions, giving preference to certain traffic or denying other traffic.[DD] The redirection server rinetd is widely available, simple to configure, and can be used to redirect, deny, and log network traffic.[EE]

In extreme cases you may opt to block outgoing SSH and HTTPS traffic. This eliminates encrypted traffic and the common routes for tunneled traffic. This is not a perfect solution, as it is possible to tunnel SSH over other protocols, but it reduces the available bandwidth and makes tunneling more challenging.

If HTTPS is essential, you can throttle the traffic back. This reduces the bandwidth available for tunneling SSH. Normal HTTPS traffic can still go through, but since tunneled traffic requires more bandwidth it increases the time required for large-scale data exfiltration, improving the odds you will detect it through network monitoring.

Detecting Protocol Tunneling

Since protocol tunneling is possible whenever you allow traffic in and out of your network, you also need to consider a detection strategy.

[BB]Some examples are the following: BalaBit IT Security (www.balabit.com/) sells Zorp, a "perimeter defense" tool for implementing application level network policies, including quality-of-service (QoS). Cisco (www.cisco.com/) includes an ALG in IOS, the operating system for much of their hardware. AEP Networks (www.aepnetworks.com/) produces SmartGate, a ALG solution.
[CC]www.squid-cache.org/
[DD]Dante is an open-source application with a variety of free and commercial modules to modify its functionality. It can be obtained from Inferno Nettverk, A/S (www.inet.no/dante).
[EE]www.boutell.com/rinetd/index.html

Monitor your network. Intrusion-detection and intrusion-prevention systems (IDS/IPS) can be used to detect suspicious traffic. A very common IDS is Snort,[FF] described more fully in the Chapter 1, "Denial of Service." This can be combined with other network monitoring software, including SANCP, a network logging and auditing tool, and Sguil, a real-time network event monitor available for most platforms.[GG]

Netfilter is a packet filtering framework for Linux.[HH] This can be combined with the L7-filters to classify packets according to protocol (HTTP, bittorrent, Kazaa, etc.), and even to detect certain kinds of protocol tunnels.[II]

THE FUTURE OF PROTOCOL TUNNELING

Attacks on network infrastructure are becoming both more focused and more financially motivated. Modern attacks may focus on extortion or espionage, rather than on simply gaining access. As financial incentives increase, so does the risk of data exfiltration by a trusted insider. Worse, employees may carry laptops home and, even though they may not have confidential information on their machines, at work they may access confidential sites and information. Malware on a compromised employee laptop can later be used to create a protocol tunnel to allow attackers into the laptop when it is connected to the company network.

The means to create protocol tunnels are becoming both more sophisticated (e.g., SSH over HTTP) and easier to deploy. The reliance on common of-the-shelf software and solutions for easily creating and managing protocol tunnels is troubling for the following reason: the user may not fully understand the implications of what they are doing. If an attacker determines that particular protocol tunneling software is being used, they may acquire the software themselves and reverse-engineer it to find vulnerabilities (or just wait for a published vulnerability to exploit). The pace of vulnerability detection and exploit far outstrips patching of software, especially on machines like laptops that are not always on, and which move around to a variety of untrusted networks.

Fortunately, the ability to detect unauthorized tunnels is improving as well. Data occupies space. The amount of space per unit of data may vary, but bits do correspond to something physical: space on a DVD, a data thumb, printed pages, or a signal on a wire. This is the basic idea of *bandwidth*. If you have to transmit one protocol over another protocol, even Transmission Control Protocol over IP, then you pay a penalty in overhead. This idea can potentially be exploited to detect covert channels.[JJ]

[FF]www.snort.org/

[GG]http://sguil.sourceforge.net/

[HH]http://netfilter.org/

[II]"L7" refers to the *application* layer in the OSI network layer model. The L7-filters can be found at http://l7-filter.sourceforge.net/.

[JJ]Annarita Giani et al. used this idea to define the *covertness* of a channel as the difference between the capacity of the channel and the transmission rate. A very low transmission rate for a high-capacity tunnel provides fewer opportunities to observe transmission. See their paper "Data Exfiltration and Covert Channels," in *Proceedings of the SPIE Defense and Security Symposium*, Orlando, Florida, April 2006.

Researchers at the University of California at San Diego have been developing a system called Glavlit to vet all information before it is allowed to leave the network to prevent data exfiltration by *either* overt or covert channels.[KK] The idea is that the only data allowed to travel out of the network is preauthorized data. Information that is to be sent out of the network is first sent to a *warden* that employs some mechanism to determine whether to allow or deny the transmission. Although this approach guarantees that data leaving the network has been vetted, it *cannot* guarantee that sensitive data is not exfiltrated using steganographic or other cloaking techniques. If the data to be transmitted is small, it can even be encoded in the delay between transmissions, or in time stamps of transmitted data. Despite this, Glavlit looks like a promising technology to prevent *bulk* data exfiltration.

Other approaches rely on detecting suspicious traffic using statistical methods. Tunnel Hunter uses statistical fingerprinting and profiling techniques to detect covert tunnels with high accuracy.[LL] Driving down the bandwidth of a covert channel does not necessarily help avoid detection with this approach. Instead, one should drive *up* the volume of legitimate (or legitimate looking) traffic in relation to the covert payload.

SUMMARY

Data exfiltration by protocol tunneling is a serious concern, and by its very nature protocol tunneling is impossible to perfectly defeat. This chapter explained how protocol tunneling is used, and detailed some of the methods for defense against this attack. You should have an understanding of why protocol tunneling is difficult to completely prevent, but also have understand basic steps you can take to protect against protocol tunneling.

[KK]Nabil Schear, Carmelo Kintana, Qing Zhang, and Amin Vahdat, "Glavlit: Preventing Exfiltration at Wire Speed." *Proceedings of the 5th ACM Workshop on Hot Topics in Networks (HotNets-V)*, November 2006.

[LL]See MD, et al., "Detection of Encrypted Tunnels Across Network Boundaries," in *Proceedings of the IEEE International Conference on Communications (ICC)*, Beijing, May 2008.

Spanning Tree Attacks

In November 2002, the staff at Beth Israel Deaconess Hospital in Boston, Massachusetts, had to be retrained to use paper records. Starting on November 13, and lasting almost 4 days, the hospital's network failed. The hospital had backup generators, second backups for those, and even batteries. They clustered their servers and performed parallel backups. They also had redundant network links, and that, sadly, caused some of the problem.

Hospitals generate and consume a lot of data in their daily operations. During this period, hospital staff, in addition to usual duties, had to ferry a quarter-million sheets of paper around the hospital. Lab results were written down, dumped in plastic bins, and delivered by runners. So, what caused this crash? It wasn't terrorism; it wasn't even malicious hackers in this case.

> *"The problem had to do with a system called* Spanning Tree Protocol *(STP), which finds the most efficient way to move information through the network and blocks alternate routes to prevent data from getting stuck in a loop."*[1]

On November 13, a researcher was uploading a large volume of data, and that triggered the underlying problem. When traffic on an Ethernet link increases, packets begin to be dropped. Among the dropped packets are those used by the STP; it starts to see the network link as "dead" and enables previously disabled links to correct the problem. A loop results, data travels around and around the loop indefinitely, and the network fails. In this case, the failure was made possible because network administrators had misconfigured their network as it had grown. The STP allows a maximum of seven "hops," or connections, between network bridges. In some cases the hospital had 10.[A]

LAYERS OF THE INTERNET

Networks are built-in *layers* to separate concerns. Each layer hides all the details of the levels below it, so engineers working at a particular level do not have to concern themselves with the levels below. At the lowest levels, engineers work with electrical or optical fields to transmit bits between hardware units. At the highest levels application programmers send complex messages between machines. Web developers don't want to understand Faraday rotators,[B] and the engineers don't want to understand SOAP.[C] Who could blame either one?

The Open Systems Interconnection (OSI) Reference Model[D] provides a seven-layer model for networks, ranging from transmitting bits at the *physical* layer to transmitting arbitrary data at the *application* layer. The seven layers of the OSI model are shown in Figure 5.1. We can broadly divide these layers into two classes: the ones that deal with the transmission medium (the "media" layers) and those that deal with messages being sent (the "host" layers). Ideally, each layer provides services to the layer immediately above it, and uses the services of the layer immediately below it. Examples of particular protocols in each layer are given on the right-hand side of Figure 5.1.

Of course this is all too organized and regimented, and in the world of the Internet this isn't actually how things work. In fact, the technical document that sets forth much of the Internet's architecture and philosophy contains a section titled "Layering Considered Harmful," in which the authors argue that rigid layering leads to inefficiency and duplication of functionality.[E] It is still necessary to know a bit about the OSI reference model to understand local area network (LAN) standards such as IEEE 802.[F] Further, the

---

[A]For a lot of detail on this, see Edwin Hoffman, "All Systems Down – Reprise (Case Study CS401)," Raptor Networks Technology, Inc. At the time of writing this document is available from http://truebit.nl/Raptor/PDF/CS401.pdf.

[B]Yes, it's a real thing. This is used to prevent light from "leaking" (because of reflection) backward through a link by changing its phase angle, thus creating an optical isolator, or "optical diode." You're welcome.

[C]SOAP is the simple object access protocol that runs (typically) atop HTTP and provides a way to pass structured data to Web services and decode the reply. For more information visit www.w3.org/TR/soap/.

[D]Hubert Zimmermann, "OSI Reference Model – The ISO Model for Architecture for Open Systems Interconnection," IEEE Transactions on Communications, vol. 28, no. 4, April 1980, pp. 425–32.

[E]RFC 3439, Section 3. A "requests for comments" (RFC) can be obtained from several sites on the Web, including www.ietf.org/rfc.html.

[F]IEEE 802 is actually a collection of standards. The Institute of Electrical and Electronics Engineers (IEEE) publishes a variety of standards for LAN and metropolitan area networks (MAN), including the well-known 802.3 for Ethernet and 802.11 a/b/g/n for wireless networks. There are many others in the collection, including specification for cable modems and Bluetooth. Visit www.ieee.org/web/standards/home for more information.

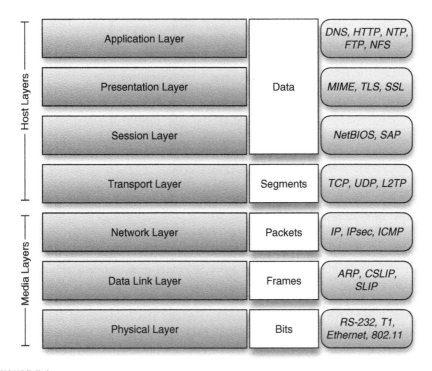

FIGURE 5.1

OSI Reference Model

literature will often refer to the data link layer as "layer two," which makes little sense unless you know about the OSI reference model (and count from the bottom).

The actual conceptual layering of the Internet is shown in Figure 5.2.[G] Note that even though some of the labels are the same, the layers aren't perfectly analogous. At the bottom level is the link layer concerned with physical connections between hardware devices (this corresponds to the combined OSI physical and data link layers).

The link layer is responsible for transmitting *frames*, well-defined collections of bits. Frames contain a preamble and a start of frame marker to allow devices to *synchronize* correctly. They also contain a cyclic redundancy check (CRC), a checksum to allow for error detection. When a frame is received the CRC is computed and compared to the value stored in the frame. If they do not match, the receiver requests that the frame be retransmitted. The frame has a *source* address and a *destination* address, but these are not Internet host names, or even the somewhat familiar Internet Protocol (IP) addresses. This level of the Internet uses Media Access

---

[G]See RFC 1122 and RFC 1123.

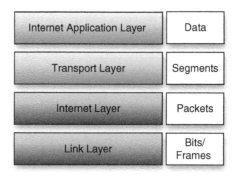

FIGURE 5.2

The Internet Protocol Suite Layers

Control (MAC) addresses, 6-byte addresses uniquely assigned to hardware.[H] An Ethernet frame contains between 46 and 1,500 bytes of actual data, along with 26 bytes of overhead.

The Internet layer is home to the IP. This is where the more familiar IP addresses are found, and where internetwork routing occurs.[I] The fundamental unit of communication at this layer is an IP *packet*. IP packets contain an IP header, specifying the source and destination IP address, and some amount of data. The packet itself is transmitted as the data component of a frame.

At the transport layer we find the Transaction Control Protocol (TCP) and User Datagram Protocol (UDP). Again we have a header for the protocol followed by the data to transmit. For TCP and UDP, this includes the source and destination *ports*, the length of the data, and another checksum. TCP provides for large messages to be broken up across multiple packets and reassembled in the correct order without duplication. To accomplish this, it includes a *sequence number* in every packet that identifies the packet's position in the overall message.

Finally, the Internet application layer provides protocols that operate on top of the TCP, such as Hypertext Transfer Protocol (HTTP) and Secure Socket Layer (SSL). In general, people working with these protocols do not need to concern themselves with how messages are delivered; since message fragmentation, reassembly, and verification are handled at the transport layer, routing is handled at the Internet layer, and the details of sending bits from one physical device to another is handled at the link layer.

[H]You've probably seen these. They consist of strings of the form 01:23:45:67:89:AB. Chunks of this address space are broken out and assigned to device manufacturers and other organizations. For instance, addresses starting 00:1B:63 are assigned to Apple Computer, Inc. The IEEE maintains this mapping. Visit http://standards.ieee.org/regauth/oui/index.shtml.

[I]IP addresses are those strings of four numbers traditionally separated by periods, such as 127.0.0.1. These are discussed in section two of Chapter 1, "Denial of Service." Mapping between IP addresses and host names, such as google.com, is handled by the Domain Name Service (DNS), an application-layer protocol.

The transmission of data on Ethernet is summarized in Figure 5.3. To transmit the Hypertext Markup Language (HTML) content of a single Web page, the message is broken into chunks to be sent and reassembled by TCP. Each TCP packet becomes the data payload of an IP packet that in turn becomes the data payload of a frame. The multiple frames are then transmitted across physical links on the Internet (across a wire, across fiber, or as a wireless signal). The term "TCP/IP" is often used as a synonym for the IP suite, as these two protocols are the most commonly used.

You start your Web browser and navigate to your *Star Trek* blog. A ha! Your "friend" Mike has commented on your latest post, a lengthy discussion of the crossover episode from *Deep Space Nine* and the original *Trek*. You click the comment to read it. Your browser creates an HTTP request and then opens a TCP connection to send it. This creates a "flood" of TCP packets that are encapsulated as IP packets and finally as frames. The frames travel from your computer to your local network, then through your cable modem or phone line to your home Internet service provider (ISP), then out onto the wider Internet. Traveling from router to router they eventually reach the ISP hosting your blog, where the frame data is extracted and passed to the IP layer, then to the TCP layer where the fragments are reassembled in order and any missing fragments are re-requested, finally resulting in an HTTP request being passed to the ISP's Web server. Then the process starts all over from the other side.

TIP

You can use a tool like **traceroute** to see the path your packets take. This utility is available under UNIX operating systems (like Solaris and Mac OS X), Linux, and Windows. On Windows the utility is named **tracert** and can be run from the command prompt. Watching how packets propagate can help you diagnose whether a problem is on your machine, your local network, your ISPs network, or somewhere else.[J]

At the time of writing, tracing the route from the University of Maryland to Google gives the output shown in Figure 5.4.[K]

There are several guides online explaining how to read the output of **traceroute** or **tracert**. Essentially what you see at each step is a host name or IP address, followed by "ping" times.[L] This is the time for a message to be acknowledged by the particular host. Higher times (in general) mean a slower connection, but you *cannot* always count on this. Traffic on the Internet is shaped and prioritized as it travels, and "ping" traffic may receive a low priority in from some hardware. Thus, at step 7 we see ping times of just over 53 ms, whereas at step 11 (further along) the ping times *drop* to under 5 ms.

[J]You can run traceroute from other machines and see what route is taken. The site www.traceroute.org/ hosts a collection of links to servers that provide publicly available traceroute functionality.

[K]See the University of Maryland's publicly available traceroute facility at http://noc.net.umd.edu/cgi-bin/traceroute/trace. A list of public traceroute servers is available from www.traceroute.org/.

[L]The actual implementation can use UDP packets or Internet control message protocol (ICMP) packets. The first is more common on UNIX, and the second is the method used by tracert on Windows at the time of writing.

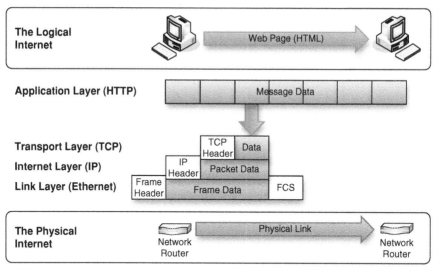

FIGURE 5.3

Sending a Web Page across Ethernet

```
 1  Vlan5.css-nts-r1.net.umd.edu (128.8.5.60)  0.571 ms
 2  Gi5-1.css-core-r1.net.umd.edu (128.8.0.9)  0.314 ms
 3  Gi3-2.css-fw-r1.net.umd.edu (128.8.0.82)  1.471 ms
 4  Gi2-1.css-max-r1.net.umd.edu (128.8.0.234)  0.468 ms
 5  clpk-umd-isp.maxgigapop.net (206.196.177.154)  0.454 ms
 6  65.120.78.45 (65.120.78.45)  1.210 ms
 7  dcp-brdr-03.inet.qwest.net (205.171.251.110)  53.082 ms
 8  xe-9-1-0.edge1.washington4.level3.net (4.68.63.81)  3.457 ms
 9  ae-2-79.edge1.Washington1.Level3.net (4.68.17.80)  15.969 ms
10  GOOGLE-INC.edge1.Washington1.Level3.net (4.79.22.38)  5.466 ms
11  209.85.241.50 (209.85.241.50)  4.822 ms
12  64.233.175.109 (64.233.175.109)  5.558 ms
13  216.239.49.149 (216.239.49.149)  5.228 ms
14  yo-in-f104.1e100.net (64.233.169.104)  5.126 ms
```

FIGURE 5.4

Traceroute Output

UNDERSTANDING THE SPANNING TREE PROTOCOL

One reason why the Internet is so reliable is that it allows for *redundancy*. Eventually physical hardware wears out and fails. People trip over power and network cables and "accidentally" unplug things they should not. Earthquakes and other natural disasters can destroy infrastructure. Construction workers dig up fiber-optic cables. Undersea cables are cut.[M] Despite all this folks, halfway around the world can still receive the

---

[M]Several undersea cables supplying Internet to countries in the Middle East were cut in 2008. So many, in fact, that suspicion arose as to whether someone was deliberately trying to disconnect these countries. See this article in Wired (retrieved November 3, 2009): www.wired.com/threatlevel/2008/12/mediterranean-c/. Because of the Internet's redundancy these cuts degrade service, but do not necessarily deny it. Satellite links and alternate routing can be used. See also this article on Engaget (retrieved November 3, 2009): www.engadget.com/2008/02/05/fourth-undersea-cable-cut-near-uae-suspicions-rise/.

wisdom of your latest blog post on six reasons why Gene Roddenberry was right the first time when he wanted to name the starship *Yorktown* instead of *Enterprise*.

Redundancy is a fundamental property of networks. Used intelligently, it allows networks to "self-heal" by detecting trouble and routing traffic around the trouble spot. This implies that there may be more than one link between any two pieces of hardware, and more than one route between any two machines. How do we choose the route a particular packet will take at any given moment?

Devices connected to the Internet can move. Are you browsing from your living room? From the coffee shop down the street? From the coffee shop next to the coffee shop down the street? From the coffee shop in an airport in a foreign country? Somehow packets intended for your machine find their way to your machine.

The Problem of Loops

This process of route discovery and packet routing takes place at several levels of the Internet, but we are concerned here with the link layer. Consider Figure 5.5. The machine Alice has MAC address 00:00:00:00:00:01, while the machine Bob has MAC address 00:00:00:00:00:02. Two switches connect these machines: switch X and switch Y. Each switch has three ports, named *p0*, *p1*, and *p2* on switch X, and *q0*, *q1*, and *q2* on switch Y. We want to send a frame from Alice to Bob.

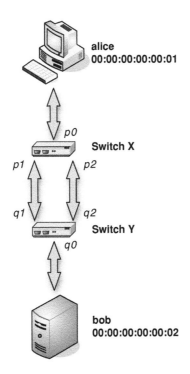

FIGURE 5.5

A Redundant Connection

> **NOTE**
>
> Router? Switch? Hub? What's the difference? Hubs allow multiple devices to share a single line. Switches connect machines to form networks. Routers connect entire networks.
>
> A *hub* connects multiple Ethernet lies to a single line, essentially creating a party line. At most one machine can talk on the line at a time. If two or more machines try to talk at the same time, we have a *collision*, and both must stop sending, wait a random amount of time, and then talk if the line appears to be idle. Essentially a hub is a dumb backbone that connects multiple lines to a single line.
>
> This situation can be improved using a *switch* that accepts frames from every port, determines the appropriate output port for each frame, and then transmits the frame on that port. A switch connects multiple lines to each other. Multiple machines can communicate at the same time, an improvement over the hub. Because this situation is more complex, switches require special internal logic to keep track of the appropriate port for each frame. Some switches also provide security and configuration features.
>
> A *router* connects networks. This is a significantly harder job, and thus routers are more complex (and more expensive) than switches. One side of a router may be an Ethernet cable, whereas on the other side there may be a Ethernet cable, phone line, serial cable, or something else. Routers often provide a rich set of configuration and security options.
>
> To return to the OSI model, we can say that hubs operate at the physical layer (layer one). Switches operate at the data link layer (layer two). Routers operate at the network layer (layer three).
>
> As a final note, be aware that these terms are not always used correctly. Sometimes what someone calls a "hub" is actually a switch or even a router. Fortunately *you* will never make that mistake.

To simplify this discussion, we will use the machine names instead of the MAC addresses. Keep in mind that the frames contain the MAC addresses, and *not* the names! When a frame arrives at a switch, we examine the frame's source and destination addresses. Initially the frame from Alice arrives at switch X, on port $p0$, with destination Bob. From this switch X learns that Alice is on port $p0$. It does not yet know where to find Bob, so it sends the frame out on *all* ports (this is called *flooding*), except the port on which it received the frame. The frame is sent on $p1$ and $p2$.

Now switch Y receives the frame from Alice to Bob, but we have a race condition. The frame might arrive on either port $q1$ or port $q2$ first. Switch Y doesn't "know" that both ports connect to the same switch; they might connect to anything, and these connections might even be changed. Suppose the frame arrives on port $q1$ first. From this frame switch Y discovers that Alice is on port $q1$. It doesn't know where to find Bob, either, so it also floods the frame to ports $q0$ and $q2$. Next the same frame arrives on port $q2$, and the process is repeated.

Meanwhile the frame from Alice to Bob arrives back at switch X on port $p2$. From this switch X concludes that Alice must be on port $p2$. It floods ports $p0$ and $p1$, and the whole process continues. These frames continue to travel around the loop created by the redundant connection. When Bob finally replies, it is too late; a perpetual loop has been created that causes the switches to constantly update their internal tables with bad information.

To avoid this condition, we need to disable one of the redundant links between the switches. Fortunately, Radia Perlman solved this problem in 1985 with the introduction of the STP,[N] and this became an IEEE standard in 1990.[O] This is a combination of an algorithm and a Link Layer Protocol that creates a loop-free view of the network. Certain redundant paths are disabled but can be re-enabled automatically if needed (so the network retains its redundancy).

Solving the Loop Problem with the Spanning Tree Protocol

In mathematical graph theory, a *spanning tree* of a graph is a subset of the graph such that all nodes are connected and there are no loops. Translated to the world of networks, a *network* spanning tree is a subset of all the network links such that no loops are formed. Returning to Figure 5.5, one way to create a spanning tree is to disable the link between *p2* and *q2*. Now when a frame from Alice to Bob arrives at switch X, it is sent on the link from *p1* to *q1*. The frame arrives at switch Y, which sends it out on port *q0*, where Bob receives the frame. Once Bob replies, the switch tables are set as shown in Tables 5.1 and 5.2. Subsequent frames are immediately sent to the correct port (no need for flooding).

It is obvious to us which links to cut in Figure 5.5 to create a loop-free path because we have a small network and we can see it all at once. The individual switches cannot "see" the network, so they need a means to communicate among themselves, determine what paths are redundant, and agree which ones to disable.

When discussing the STP, devices that connect network links are called *bridges*. They may be routers, switches, wireless access points, or other machines that act as routers or switches. Bridges in a network use special frames called *bridge protocol data units* (BPDU frames) to exchange information as they try to compute the spanning tree. Three kinds of BPDU frames are typically used:

Table 5.1 Switch X table	
Switch X	
00:00:00:00:00:01 (Alice)	*p0*
00:00:00:00:00:02 (Bob)	*p1*

Table 5.2 Switch Y table	
Switch Y	
00:00:00:00:00:01 (Alice)	*q1*
00:00:00:00:00:02 (Bob)	*q0*

[N]Perlman, R., "An Algorithm for Distributed Computation of a Spanning Tree in an Extended LAN," ACM SIGCOMM Computer Communication Review, volume 15, number 4, pages 44–53, 1985.
[O]IEEE 802.1D.

- A *configuration* BPDU (CBPDU) is used to compute the spanning tree.
- A *topology change notification* (TCN) BPDU is used to announce changes in the network's structure (such as when links are added or removed).
- A *topology change notification acknowledgment* (TCA) BPDU is used to respond to TCN frames and confirms their receipt.

BPDU frames are always being exchanged (usually every 2 seconds, called the *hello interval*) to keep the network information up to date.

To centralize information about the network, a particular bridge is selected and made the *root* bridge. This bridge coordinates updates to the network structure. The first task of STP is to select the root bridge. Every bridge has a 2-byte priority assigned to it (a number in the range 0 to 65,535). The network administrator can change this priority. Every bridge also has a unique 6-byte MAC address. The combination of these two numbers is the 8-byte *bridge identifier* (BID).[P] This is used to determine the root bridge in the following manner: the bridge with the lowest priority is the root bridge. If two or more bridges have equal priority, then the bridge with the lowest MAC address will be the root bridge.

The implementation of this is simple: every bridge floods a BPDU containing its BID and announcing that it is the root bridge.[Q] If a bridge receives a frame with a lower BID, then it knows it cannot be the root bridge, and it stops generating these frames. Otherwise it continues, since it may be the root bridge. Ultimately only one bridge is generating frames claiming to be the root bridge: the bridge with the lowest BID.

Every other bridge needs a unique path to the root bridge. Because communication with the root bridge is frequent, this path should be a *least-cost* path. The cost of traversing a link is determined by the version of the STP protocol in use, the data rate, and the settings applied by the network administrator. Once the root bridge has been chosen, every other bridge computes the cost of each path from itself to the root, and chooses the least-cost path. The port that corresponds to the least-cost path is known as the *root port*. For each network link the bridges on the ends of the link determine which of them has the least-cost path to the root. The port connecting the least-cost bridge to the network link becomes the *designated port* for that particular link. After the costs are computed and bridge and designated ports are chosen, all other ports are blocked. At this point, the loop-free network has been created.

Again, the implementation of this is fairly simple. Every BPDU contains an accumulated cost. BPDU frames sent from the root bridge have their cost set to

---

[P]Like nearly everything in the world of networking, this is all true, except when it isn't. The introduction of the virtual LAN (VLAN) changes many elements of this, and the protocol itself has undergone revisions and modifications to make it faster and to add proprietary information. Covering all these details would require a much longer chapter. Still, the basic implementation of the algorithm (find a root bridge, compute the lowest-cost paths, etc.) remains the same.

[Q]Frames have a destination and source. The source is the MAC address of the sender, and the destination is a special MAC address reserved for broadcast BPDU. The particular address depends on the particular standard being used, but the IEEE STP standard specifies 01:80:C2:00:00:00.

zero. Whenever a bridge receives a BPDU frame, it adds the cost associated with the port to that frame's cost before passing it along. When BPDU frames are received on multiple ports by a bridge, the ports receiving the highest-cost frames are placed in *blocked* state, logically disabling them. This process converges (quickly or slowly, depending on many factors, but typically in under a minute) to the loop-free spanning tree.

It is possible to have ties. Multiple paths might have identical (lowest) cost. In this case the path connecting to the lowest BID is chosen. For a particular network link, multiple bridges on the link might have identical (lowest) cost. Again, these ties are broken in favor of the lowest BID. Finally, as in Figure 5.5, there may be multiple links joining two bridges. In this case, the lowest port priority wins (ports on a switch are assigned unique priorities).

From the point of view of a particular port, the process looks something like the following: initially the port is turned off, or *disabled*. When it is turned on (because its bridge is connected and turned on) it transitions to the *blocked* state, where it discards all traffic *except* BPDU frames. The port then *listens* to the BPDU frames as described earlier to identify the root bridge and build the loop-free network. A port may be *learning* about the network. In this state data frames are not forwarded, but they are examined to build the routing table. Finally, a port may be *forwarding*, in which case data frames received are routed along, and the port is "fully open." Ports transition from listening and learning states to forwarding states after a specified *forwarding delay*.

After this initial creation of a loop-free network, BPDU frames continue to be exchanged (at every hello interval) to account for updates in the network, such as a port or link failure or the addition of new hardware. It is possible, for instance, that a new switch will be added that has a BID lower than the current root bridge. It is also possible that a network administrator will alter the priorities of existing bridges. In these cases, the spanning tree must be recomputed. It is this process that can be hijacked by an intruder to cause mischief.

Finally, TCN frames are sent whenever a bridge observes a link or port being enabled or disabled. These frames are forwarded to the root bridge (so they are seen by all bridges along the path to the root), and every bridge along the way acknowledges the TCN with a TCA. This allows the necessary reconfiguration of the network when a link fails or is added, and preserves redundancy and resiliency of the network.

In a network that has converged to a loop-free state so that ports are forwarding traffic, the root bridge continues to send BPDU frames at every hello interval. These frames contain an "age" field that is initialized to zero by the root bridge and set to the time of transit of the frame as it makes its way through the network. When another bridge receives one of these frames on a port, it initializes an internal clock for that port to the provided age and begins counting up. For example, if the age is 5 seconds, the port clock will start counting from 5 seconds. If the timer reaches the configured maximum age (typically 20 seconds), then the bridge assumes that connectivity may have failed and restarts the election process for the root bridge by announcing that it is the root (the first step of the election process). After all, it is possible that the old root bridge has failed. Once the boss has left the building *someone* has to be in charge. Why not you?

HOW SPANNING TREE ATTACKS WORK

An attacker who is physically connected to your network and who has the ability to create BPDU frames with specific characteristics can use the STP to cause various kinds of havoc, from stealing data to disrupting your network (a denial of service, as described in Chapter 1, "Denial of Service"). This section describes how some of these attacks can be accomplished.

"Ah ha!" you may say. "You said 'physically connected.' We're totally secure." Well, maybe. First, there is always the risk of a malicious insider. That is, someone who routinely has access to your hardware might not be entirely without guile.[R] Second, wireless access points can broadcast BPDU frames and participate in the STP. By listening for these frames (typically broadcast by a misconfigured wireless access point), an intruder can obtain information about the network and inject their own forged BPDU frames to cause havoc. Third, have you read the rest of this book? If an attacker sitting comfortably in their parents' basement hundreds of miles away breaks into your network and compromises a machine, then they *have* a machine physically connected to your network.

Another element to note is that sometimes you have no option but to allow people to physically connect to your network. Hotels and universities, for instance, typically provide direct physical connections for guests and students, respectively. "Guests and students" covers a lot of humanity. It is worth taking steps to protect your level 2 infrastructures, as everything else is built on top of them.

Capturing BPDU Traffic

Some of the attacks described here require capturing some of the BPDU frames and examining them to determine, for instance, the current root bridge's BID. This section presents two tools to help you do this: tcpdump and Wireshark, both of which were also discussed (very briefly) in Chapter 1, "Denial of Service." Another tool, Yersinia, is described in the section Forging BPDU Packets.

tcpdump

The workhorse for capturing packets crossing an interface of your computer is a program called tcpdump.[S] This is a command-line utility for capturing and examining packets on a network interface. While tcpdump is a UNIX/Linux program, it has

---

[R]Visit www.cert.org/insider_threat/ for CERT's research on insider threat, and also http://www.thei3p .org/research/insider_threat.html for the Institute for Information Infrastructure Protection.
[S]See www.tcpdump.org/ for both tcpdump and libpcap.

been ported to Windows as WinDump.[T] In addition, you can use the packet capture facilities of tcpdump via its companion library, libpcap.

Using tcpdump is a good way to learn about a network. You can watch all the traffic, or select just certain kinds of packets to display. The full details of using tcpdump are beyond the scope of this chapter, but the following is a quick example of using tcpdump to examine STP traffic.

```
$ tcpdump -c 1 -i en0 stp
listening on en0, link-type EN10MB (Ethernet), capture size 65535
    bytes
02:28:55.673633 STP 802.1w, Rapid STP, Flags [Learn, Forward,
    Agreement], bridge-id 8000.00:01:23:45:67:89.803a, length 47
```

Here we have told tcpdump to examine traffic on the first Ethernet interface of our OS X-based Mac (**-i en0**) and to capture just one packet and stop (**-c 1**). We are only interested in STP-related traffic, so we include the **stp** filter at the end of the command. The output consists of several pieces of information. The first part of the output is a time stamp (02:28:55.673633) indicating a time of 2:28 A.M. (a good time to be up hacking). Following this we see that this packet is using the STP version defined by IEEE standard 802.1w, otherwise known as the Rapid Spanning Tree Protocol (RSTP). This is a version of the protocol that responds to topology changes (links being added and removed) much faster than the original STP standard. We are told about the port flags (the port is learning MAC addresses and forwarding frames) and the BID. The bridge has MAC address 00:01:23:45:67:89 and hexadecimal priority 8000 (or 32,768 decimal). This is the *default* bridge priority, and you are likely to see it for most of the bridges you encounter in a network.

Additional switches will cause tcpdump to generate even more detailed information, including a list of the value of every byte of the frame. Depending on where your machine is sitting in the network (you are acting as a switch, or are a PC sitting at an endpoint) you may see traffic from just one or perhaps several bridges.

Wireshark

Although tcpdump is powerful and effective (and you really should know how to use it and read its output), it is a command-line tool with a lot of cryptic switches. Can't someone package all this up in a nice graphical user interface (GUI)? Formerly known as Ethereal, Wireshark[U] is a program for capturing and decoding packets on a network interface, just as with tcpdump. Unlike tcpdump, however, Wireshark allows you to perform captures from within a (relatively) comfortable GUI. The Wireshark GUI at startup (running under Linux in this case) is shown in Figure 5.6.

Wireshark is *very* useful if you are trying to understand a Network Protocol. Figure 5.7 shows a packet capture filtered to just show STP packets (this time running on an Apple Mac). At the top of the window is the list of packets captured,

---

[T]See www.winpcap.org/windump/.
[U]See www.wireshark.org/.

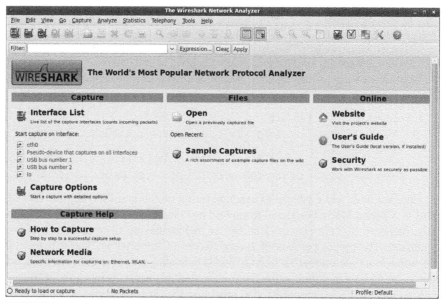

FIGURE 5.6

Wireshark

each of which is decoded. In this list, the MAC address is decoded to show the OUI (in this case the MAC is registered to 3com), followed by the unique device address. In the middle section the parts of the frame are broken out hierarchically, and decoded. In the figure, the BPDU flags section is selected, showing how the bits (01111100 in binary) are decoded. At the bottom the raw frame data is shown in hexadecimal. Since the flags section is selected, the byte containing those bits is highlighted (7C in hexadecimal). This kind of information is invaluable if you are trying to observe, understand, and then exploit a protocol.

Taking over the Root Bridge

So what can you do with the STP? One fun activity is to make your machine the root bridge. Doing this is not really hard, you simply need to forge a BPDU frame with BID that will win the root election. Remember that STP uses the bridge MAC address and the bridge priority to determine who should be the root bridge. Thus if you can detect the current root bridge and send a frame with the same priority but a *lower* MAC address, you will become the new root bridge.

For example, you might fire up Wireshark and observe STP packets for a while. As you see in Figure 5.7, the root bridge is identified, and its priority and MAC address are displayed. Suppose you see that the root bridge has priority 32,768 (the default priority) and MAC address 00:01:23:45:67:89. Now to become the root

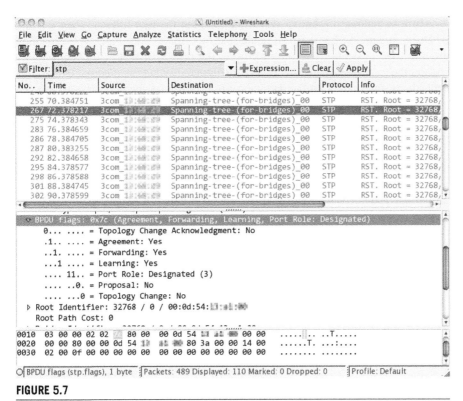

FIGURE 5.7

STP Packet Capture in Wireshark

bridge and win the next election you can broadcast BPDU status frames with a priority of 32,768 and a forged, or "spoofed" MAC address of 00:01:23:45:67:88. This lower MAC address guarantees that you will win the next election to become the root bridge. You should send these frames every 2 seconds (the "hello" interval). Of course, if you are feeling adventurous you might just set the priority to 0 and the MAC address to 00:00:00:00:00:00. In some cases this will work, too.

Denial of Service

Now that you own the root bridge, what's next? Well, recall that the root bridge is responsible for sending out BPDU frames at every hello interval. One possibility is simply to not do that, and wait for another root bridge election. When the election happens (you receive BPDU frames from a neighbor asserting themselves as the root bridge) you immediately assert yourself as root again, and win. If the maximum age is low enough and you repeat this process, you can keep the network from converging and disrupt traffic, an effective denial of service attack. An alternative is to remain the root bridge, but never send a TCA when a TCN is received. In this case, a switch's forwarding table ages rapidly and the switch must flood its ports.

There is nothing preventing you from claiming the root role and then sending BPDU configuration frames to surrender the root role. For example, you can claim the root role, then raise your priority to let the prior root win. Then immediately reclaim the root role. Again, this is very disruptive. If you time it correctly (and this depends to some extent on the particular timer values for the network—which you can see using Wireshark), you can keep several of the switches from ever transitioning their ports to a forwarding state.

Since you are lying about your MAC address, you might as well lie often. Watch for a BPDU from the current root, and then start sending BPDU frames with a MAC address one lower at the same priority. You'll win the election and become the root bridge. Now immediately decrement the MAC address and repeat. You'll become the root bridge again, but since the MAC address is different it is as if another physical machine were becoming the root bridge. Every switch must recompute its path to root and costs. Now decrement the MAC address and repeat. If you reach the lowest MAC address possible (00:00:00:00:00:00), return to the first value you used and start the cycle over. In this manner, you will keep the network in a state of eternal elections and prevent it from ever converging and transmitting traffic.

Man in the Middle

Sure, denial of service is fun and all, but what you really want to do is steal data. Depending on how much access you have in the network, you may be able to do just that. Remember that STP is responsible for determining which links are blocked and which are active. Since data travels only on active links, you may be able to create a situation in which most or all of the network traffic you care about is routed through your machine. You can then capture it (using tcpdump, Wireshark, or a custom program built using libpcap) and sift through it at your leisure.

Doing this requires having connections to two switches such that the data you want is going to be passing between them. This situation is shown in Figure 5.8. Here traffic between Alice and Bob typically passes between switches A and B (not necessarily a direct link). The intruder connects to the physical network (not necessarily directly to switches A and B) such that he or she has an alternate route between Alice and Bob, and then begins sending BPDU frames so that his or her ports become the designated ports for traffic. This would create a loop, but fortunately STP steps in and all other links between switches A and B are disabled. Now all traffic between Alice and Bob will be routed through the intruder's machine.

The important thing to realize about this attack is that if the intruder has sufficient knowledge of the network, then they do *not* necessarily have to have direct access to switches A and B to pull this off. The intruder simply has to generate a configuration that results in the path through it winning over the direct path from A to B. After all, if the intruder did have direct access to the two switches, they might be able to simply physically insert themselves by plugging and unplugging cables.

One way to accomplish this is shown in Figure 5.9. Here the intruder has access to two other bridges: C and D. (It is even possible these could be wireless access

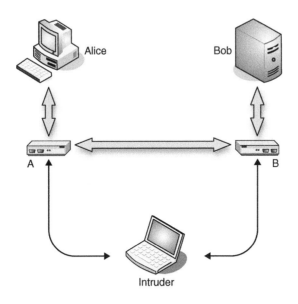

FIGURE 5.8

Man in the Middle Attack

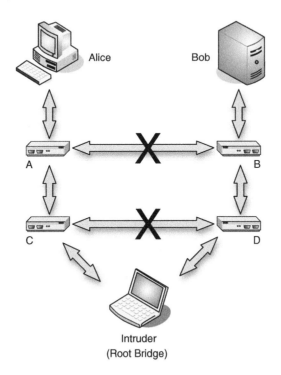

FIGURE 5.9

Alternate Man in the Middle Attack

points that have been misconfigured to forward BPDU frames.) The attacker claims the root bridge role, and now every bridge computes the least-cost path to the root. The least-cost paths from C and D are most likely the direct links, and thus cannot be blocked. Thus, any other link between A and B and any other link between C and D must be blocked to prevent cycles. Now the intruder is free to watch the traffic.

Forging BPDU Frames

The key to hijacking the STP is forging BPDU frames. If you can construct and send BPDU frames with specific characteristics, you can cause havoc with the protocol because layer two is essentially security-free.

If you are a programmer, you can use the libnet library[V] to construct and send BPDU frames. This is a networking library that lets you programmatically access several protocols. Libnet is a relatively low-level library, allowing you to specially craft and then send packets. For example, you might create and send configuration STP packets (BPDU frames) in an attempt to claim the root bridge role for yourself. Using libnet requires that you write a program. While libnet is a C library, helpful people have created other interfaces to it, including a Perl library[W] and Python library.[X] In short, the library is highly available.

Of course, this is the twenty-first century, and you've got other things to think about. Can't someone else do the work for you? Of course they can. A whole variety of layer 2 attacks (not just spanning tree attacks) is available using a tool called *Yersinia*,[Y] a freely available, open-source tool for launching certain network protocol attacks, including against STP. At the time of writing, Yersinia has a "curses" interface (that is, it has a text-based GUI), but an even nicer GUI is in development. After all, STP is already hard enough, isn't it? The Yersinia GUI is shown in Figure 5.10. Note that while Yersinia runs under Linux and UNIX (including Mac OS X), it is not available for Windows at the time of writing.

Now that you have Yersinia, you are ready to launch some attacks. Pressing **h** brings up the quick help, and pressing **x** brings up the list of available attacks (shown in Figure 5.10). Note that at the bottom of the display is a list of the STP fields. These can be edited directly by typing **e**, and allow you to craft whatever STP packet you wish. Also note that you can explicitly claim the root bridge role or relinquish it ("claiming other role") from this interface, as well as launch a variety of denial of service attacks (those attacks with an *X* in the DoS column). There really isn't much more to it.

[V] See http://libnet.sourceforge.net/.

[W] For Perl, see www.perl.org/. The Perl interface to libnet is Net::Libnet; see http://search.cpan.org/~smpeters/Net-Libnet-0.01_03/lib/Net/Libnet.pm.

[X] For Python, see http://python.org/. The Python interface to libnet is pylibnet; see http://pylibnet.sourceforge.net/.

[Y] See www.yersinia.net/. For the record, yersinia pestis is the bacterium associated with the bubonic plague. See how network security can be a fun learning experience?

FIGURE 5.10

Yersinia's Text-based GUI

> **WARNING**
>
> You may be tempted to experiment with these tools on your home network. You might even be tempted to experiment with them on your ISP's network, or your work network. Unless you are a network administrator or you are performing penetration testing, you might want to be careful. Many networks are monitored for aggressive port scanning, and it probably violates the terms of service. Technologies like BPDU guard (explained later) can actually result in your connection being severed and requiring a manual reset.

Discovering the Network

How does an attacker come to understand your network topology? For that matter, how can you keep track of it? Using libpcap, you can capture network traffic and analyze it to try to deduce a network topology. If that sounds like programming, take heart: someone has built tools to do this for you.

One useful tool is EtherApe.[Z] If you can collect packets (using tcpdump or Wireshark), you can even use EtherApe offline. The trick is to find machines that give you a good view of the network, and capture packets on those machines. You

---

[Z]See http://etherape.sourceforge.net/.

can then use EtherApe with the captured packet files to see the overall structure of the network and plan your attack (or defense). Figure 5.11 shows EtherApe running. The circles are network nodes (their size is related to the amount of traffic), and the lines are particular directed flows (their width is related to the amount of traffic). Colors are used on the interface to indicate particular protocols.

You can capture traffic using tcpdump and then use EtherApe to visualize this traffic. To do this, you need to run tcpdump with the **–n** flag (to prevent name resolution) and the **–w** flag (to specify a capture file). The following is an example.

```
$ tcpdump -n -c 1000 -w network.pcap
```

This will capture 1,000 packets and write them to the **network.pcap** file. You can then tell EtherApe to read this file as input (instead of trying to read network traffic on the local machine) via the **–r** switch.

```
$ etherape -F -z -r network.pcap
```

EtherApe is designed to watch traffic in near real time. The **–F** indicates that old traffic lines should not fade, and the **–z** indicates that EtherApe shouldn't replay the traffic using the time stamps, but just display the diagram. Note that you can configure EtherApe to display only data from a particular protocol layer, such as the link layer (layer two), which is what is being shown in Figure 5.11. EtherApe does not

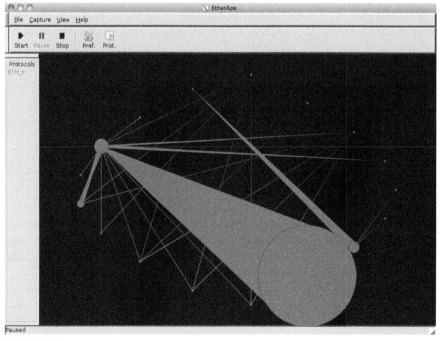

FIGURE 5.11

EtherApe

attempt to show you the network topology, *per se*, but it does show you flows in the network and does help you discover other hosts.

Nmap is an open-source network-mapping tool. Nmap provides a GUI called Zenmap that can help visualize your network. Unlike EtherApe, you give Nmap a list of hosts to scan, and it builds its data by actively scanning the hosts (instead of passively sniffing packets). This allows you to detect not only what hosts are available, but in many cases what the hosts *do*, as Nmap gives you a list of interesting ports that are open on the host. The Zenmap GUI provides the "topology" view shown in Figure 5.12. The Nmap tool is described in Chapter 1, "Denial of Service."

There are other utilities, as well, including commercial utilities like Lumeta's IPsonar[AA] and SolarWinds LANsurveyor,[BB] and freeware applications like LanToplog.[CC]

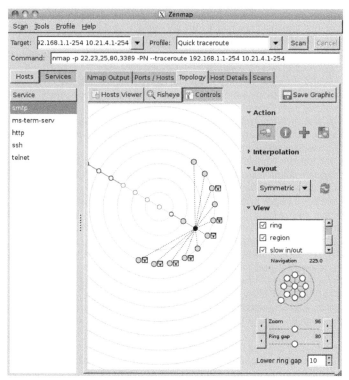

FIGURE 5.12

Zenmap's Topology View

[AA]See www.lumeta.com/ipsonar/.
[BB]See www.solarwinds.com/products/LANsurveyor/.
[CC]See www.lantopolog.com/download.html.

DANGERS OF SPANNING TREE ATTACKS

Spanning tree attacks can cause havoc at the link level of your network. This is very disruptive; switches can stop sending any packets at all, so it becomes difficult to get information from network monitoring software.

If intruders can insert themselves into your network and capture packets, they can subvert many network security assumptions. Some organizations use unencrypted e-mail connections with clear-text authentication. After all, it is impossible to connect to the mail server unless one is physically connected to the network or connected using an encrypted virtual private network (VPN) connection. Of course, an

---

EPIC FAIL

The Beth Israel Deaconess Hospital failure is a very interesting case study. In particular, it is worth considering the actions of the network administrators as they tried to alleviate the problem.

When network administrators noticed the network acting sluggishly they decided to act in a very "reasonable" fashion; they would shut down switches one by one until they located the source of the trouble. If the network trouble cleared up, then they would have localized the problem and could diagnose and fix it.

As they shut down switches, they forced the recalculation of the spanning tree. The switches were now spending all their time recalculating the spanning tree, and never entering the forwarding state. The network stopped routing any traffic except the layer 2 packets. The situation was *not* simply reversible. Turning all switches back on did not restore the previous network state; it created a situation in which the network would *sometimes* route traffic, and sometimes not route traffic at all.

Finally, the network admins diagnosed the problem as a loop in the STP. They began shutting down redundant links in the network to restore order. As they worked late into the night, the network settled down. The problem was fixed...until the next day.

The network had begun routing traffic, it turns out, because it was late at night and very few people were using it. The next morning as hospital activity increased, the network resumed its chaotic working/slow/dead cycle. As the day went on the network admins kept trying reasonable tactics to restore the network, always feeling they were just about to fix the problem. The hospital had to shut down its emergency room. All over the hospital critical lab reports were delayed. Knowing that the network admins were "just about to fix the problem" wasn't helping. The hospital management team essentially declared an emergency, and called Cisco Systems.

Cisco set up a command center at the hospital and began an aggressive plan to solve the problem. From 6 P.M. until 9 A.M. the next day, the Cisco team worked to diagnose the problem, and eventually found the problematic loop. New hardware was delivered, and the network rebuilt, again working late into the night. The problem was fixed—until the next day.

It took a few more days to restore the network, as more loops were found and fixed. There are many lessons to be taken from this case, ranging from keeping up-to-date physical and logical network diagrams to planning for eating and sleeping arrangements for your network team in the event of a disaster.[DD]

[DD]For a good discussion of the lessons learned, see Scott Berinato, "All Systems Down," CIO, 11 April 2003. At the time of writing, this article was available online at www.cio.com.au/article/65115/all_systems_down.

attacker who can manipulate the spanning tree to observe all packets can then capture e-mail account passwords. Do you use different passwords for all your accounts? Do your system administrators send you certificates and keys via e-mail?

DEFENDING AGAINST SPANNING TREE ATTACKS

Unlike the other attacks described in this book, spanning tree attacks require that the attacker have access to a machine physically connected to your network. Thus, the first line of defense is to make sure that all your network hardware is properly configured and that only those people who need access to the hardware have access. Next, you need to take steps to prevent intruders from gaining remote access to your network, as remote access is the next best thing to being there. Finally, it is worth observing your network from time to time to see what is actually happening. You can use the Cisco IOS *show spanning-tree* command for this purpose.

Disable STP

One simple approach is to disable STP when it is not needed. For example, if you have a physically loop-free network (and thus no redundancy), you have no need for STP. Small networks using a single switch, or just a few switches without any physical loops, can have STP disabled altogether. Of course since your network has no redundant loops, failure of a single link may cause complete failure of some portion of your network.

An alternative is to allow redundant network connections between switches, but to use *link aggregation* instead of STP. Link aggregation has been implemented by many different vendors, and so it goes by many different names, including network interface card (NIC) teaming, port teaming, link bundling, NIC bonding, and network fault tolerance, to name a few. Fortunately, the IEEE has published a standard for link aggregation[EE] and modern hardware conforms. Of course, you are restricted in how you connect the network.

Root Guard and BPDU Guard

Cisco supports protection systems called *root guard* and *BPDU guard*.[FF] These allow one to enforce a perimeter around a network to prevent STP attacks.

Root guard is enabled and disabled on a per-port basis. Enabling root guard on a port prevents that port from becoming the root port; it may only be a designated port. When an intruder sends "superior" BPDU configuration frames attempting to claim the root bridge role, the root guard protected port is placed in a "root

---

[EE]See IEEE 802.3 (March 2000) and IEEE 802.1AX-2008 (November 2008), both of which are available from http://standards.ieee.org/.
[FF]See www.cisco.com/en/US/tech/tk389/tk621/tech_tech_notes_list.html.

inconsistent" state, during which it listens but does not forward traffic – it is blocked. Once the superior frames stop arriving, the port transitions to learning and finally to forwarding. If the superior frames start arriving again the port is blocked again.

This assures that the root bridge can never be located off of a port with root guard enabled. By correctly configuring ports with root guard, the network administrator can define the network perimeter and prevent stealing the root bridge role.

BPDU guard is another Cisco technology for defining a network perimeter and protecting against STP attacks. Like root guard, BPDU guard is enabled or disabled on a port-by-port basis. BPDU guard operates in a much more strict fashion than root guard: if a BPDU frame arrives then the port is transitioned to an "error disable" (blocked) state and generates a message about the event. Unlike root guard, the port does not automatically transition back to a forwarding state as soon as possible, but remains in the blocked state until either the state is manually cleared or an automatic recovery timer expires. Automatic recovery requires a *minimum* of 30 seconds, making denial of service attacks impractical. BPDU guard allows the network administrator to establish the limits of the STP protocol, so that BPDU frames are simply not accepted outside a defined perimeter.

BPDU guard is a good choice for ports where endpoints (workstations, printers and servers) are going to be attacked, since these devices should not be sending BPDU frames at all, unless they are explicitly configured to act as a router. BPDU guard is often combined with the *portfast* setting, which instructs a port to skip the listening and learning states and move directly to forwarding. Again, this makes sense for ports where endpoints that do *not* send BPDU frames are going to be located.

THE FUTURE OF SPANNING TREE ATTACKS

Root guard and BPDU guard are both very effective strategies to mitigate STP attacks but are both (at the time of writing) limited to Cisco hardware. These technologies may still allow an intruder to monitor BPDU frames and use these to discover network information. Once you have established a perimeter, the intruder may seek to compromise a device *inside* the perimeter. By capturing frames, an intruder can obtain the MAC addresses of devices inside the perimeter. By using other layer 2 attacks, the attacker may be able to compromise a device inside the perimeter and then launch an STP-based attack such as a denial of service.

Many different versions of STP exist with proprietary extensions, such as the *portfast* extension mentioned previously. It may be possible to exploit these extensions in ways not described here. If an intruder can set *all* ports to forward then they can force cycles and trigger a denial of service. Many switch implementations provide diagnostic settings that copy traffic from all ports to a single port, making it much easier to monitor and steal data.

STP attacks are themselves relatively new, having been initially proposed in *Phrack*[GG] magazine in 2002, and investigated at Black Hat Europe[HH] in 2005 with the introduction of Yersinia. Because of this it is likely that intruders have not yet begun to take full advantage of STP-based attacks. We can expect this sort of attack to become more prevalent.

SUMMARY

Because layer two in general, and the STP in particular, have no inherent security, layer 2 attacks will continue and pose a serious risk to network security. Other protocols exist at layer two and these can also be exploited; many of these exploits are already implemented in Yersinia. Since layer two creates the foundation for your entire network, any trouble on this level can be difficult to diagnose and can manifest itself in several ways. The incident detailed at the start of this chapter illustrates the trouble that can arise, or that an intruder can cause, using a layer 2 protocol such as STP.

This chapter explained what layer two is and investigated STP in particular. You should understand the basics of how STP operates, and how you can exploit it for denial of service and other attacks. Finally, you should understand the role of layer 2 security and the steps you can take to defend against STP exploits.

Endnote

1. Anne B. Got Paper? Beth Israel Deaconess Copes with a Massive Computer Crash. *Boston Globe*, November 26, 2002.

[GG]See www.phrack.org/. Archives are available online at this site.
[HH]David Barroso and Alfredo Omella, Yersinia, A Framework For Layer 2 Attacks, Black Hat Europe, 2005. See http://www.blackhat.com/html/bh-europe-05/bh-eu-05-speakers.html.

Man-in-the-Middle

INFORMATION IN THIS CHAPTER

- How Man-in-the-Middle Attacks Work
- Dangers with Man-in-the-Middle Attacks
- Future of Man-in-the-Middle Attacks
- Defenses against Man-in-the-Middle Attacks

Man-in-the-middle (MITM) attacks have been one of the most successful attack vectors for attackers for quite some time. The concept is old, but new methods of attack continue to surface as new technologies are developed and techniques are discovered. In short, MITM attacks are the act of unauthorized individuals or parties placing themselves in the path of a communication to eavesdrop, intercept, and possibly modify legitimate communications. Although the focus of this chapter is how MITM attacks apply to computing resources, examples of these attacks stretch back for centuries.

A classic and easy to relate to type of MITM attack could be experienced by playing a game of "telephone" like many of us did as children. A few children would sit in a line next to one another with the game starting at one end and finishing at the other end. The first child in line would whisper a message to the next child in the line. The child receiving the message would then repeat the message to the next person in line. This would occur until the message eventually reached the last person. However, sometimes, kids can be mischievous and alter the message as it travels down the line. Finally, the last person in the line would stand up and say the message received out loud. The actual message received may sometimes vary greatly from the original message. If the original message was "The chair is blue," it would be pretty funny if the final message received was "I have blue hair." Well, it would be funny if you were 8 years old.

Another example of an attack still in use today is wiretapping. Traditionally, wiretapping has been the act of eavesdropping on phone conversations by using an electronic "tap" to place the attacker on the same communication path as the

> **NOTE**
>
> The term man-in-the-middle has been used for quite some time by the network security industry; however, this type of attack has many other nicknames as well. Some of the other nicknames for this attack include monkey-in-the-middle, bucket-brigade attack, session hijacking, and Transmission Control Protocol (TCP) hijacking.

telephone being monitored. This allows the attacker to monitor and record conversations as they occur. Recording the conversations allows the attacker to review the conversations at a later time or use the recorded conversation for other reasons such as evidence or extortion.

Wiretapping may also be used by law enforcement and government organizations. During the presidency of George W. Bush, the National Security Agency (NSA) was authorized to conduct warrantless wiretapping[A] of phone conversations, e-mail, and other media for the purpose of monitoring suspected al-Qaeda communications. This type of monitoring serves as an example of how wiretapping can be used in various situations.

Attackers have been able to learn from the techniques and successes of traditional wiretapping and extend the attack vectors by applying the concept to monitor network traffic. When we observe the similarities between wiretapping as it applies to a traditional phone system and MITM attacks on networks, we can identify with and appreciate the threats associated with such attacks. Discussions of the impact of MITM and wiretapping and their impact on confidentiality and integrity are explored later in the section "Dangers with Man-in-the-Middle attacks."

One of the fundamental concepts of MITM attacks that make them so dangerous is the fact that there is virtually no reliance on operating system or network-specific vulnerabilities to perform these types of attacks. In other words, even though all your operating systems and network-enabled devices are 100 percent up to date with the manufacturer's patches, they can still be exploited by using MITM attacks in many situations. For this reason, MITM attacks can prove to be a lucrative attack avenue for attackers who wish to access sensitive information. Many vendors and working organizations have identified this threat and have slowly implemented features to hinder successful execution of these attacks. Examples of some of the controls and defensive strategies to prevent or reduce the likelihood of MITM attacks are covered in the section "Defenses against Man-in-the-Middle Attacks."

HOW MAN-IN-THE-MIDDLE ATTACKS WORK

A MITM attack can be accomplished by a variety of techniques, depending on the access the attacker has to the target network and the types of protocols being used to facilitate the attack. As a review, a MITM attack occurs when an attacker injects

---

[A]www.cnn.com/2005/POLITICS/12/17/bush.nsa/

himself or herself between one or more communication endpoints or redirects legitimate network traffic in an attempt to eavesdrop on data communications as they occur on the network or other communications platform.

Figure 6.1 provides an overview of the anatomy of a MITM attack. Although the figure is simple in its illustration of the concept, the goal is to provide a glance of what a classic MITM attack scenario may look like. In Figure 6.1, the regular flow of data is depicted by the solid lines going to and from a chat server. Normally, communications from the user to the chat server would be accomplished by sending data from the user's computer through the router and then traverse the network backbone until it establishes communications with the chat server. Once the protocols have negotiated the connection requirements, the chat client and the chat server can begin transmitting data back and forth to each other so users can communicate. Normal setup and communications only takes a few seconds to occur before users can start chatting.

In a MITM attack, represented by the broken lines in Figure 6.1, the attacker will use various techniques to reroute data between a user and the chat server. Ultimately, the attacker wants to make all communications pass through his or her computer, so he or she can sniff or modify the data while it is in transit. First, the attacker will carry out an attack to fool the user's computer into thinking the attacker's computer is the router. Then, the attacker will perform another attack to fool the router into thinking the attacker's computer is the user's computer. Once the attacker has

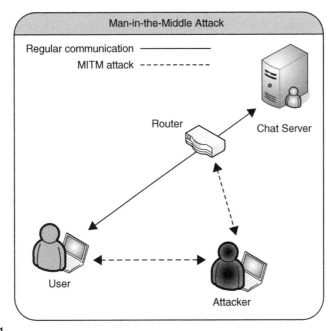

FIGURE 6.1

MITM Overview

performed these attacks against both the user's computer and the router, all the data intended to be transmitted between the router and the user's computer will be routed through the attacker's computer. The attacker now has the capability of sniffing and modifying the data intended to be viewed only by the user, router, and chat server. Although this method of attack sounds complex, the availability of several different tools makes it very easy to accomplish by even the lesser experienced attacker. Some of the tools and techniques used to perform MITM attacks are discussed later in the section "Dangers with Man-in-the-Middle Attacks."

Once an attacker has been able to successfully insert himself or herself into the communication stream, he or she is capable of performing a variety of attacks. These attacks may include sniffing network traffic, command injection, malicious code injection, and public-key cryptosystem attacks. Although several attacks have been mentioned, many more can be used by an attacker depending on the purpose of his or her attack.

Sniffing Network Traffic

Sniffing is perhaps one of the most common and least complicated types of attacks initiated after a successful MITM attack is executed. As outlined in Figure 6.1, an attacker can inject himself or herself between a target user or system and a router to view all traffic passing between the two points. As communications between the systems continue, the attacker can use tools to identify user credentials and many other types of sensitive data. Upon capturing valid credentials, the attacker may use the credentials to access services within the network only available to authenticated individuals.

Replay Attacks

Replay attacks can also be conducted as a result of successful sniffing attacks performed during MITM. A simple scenario involves capturing network traffic between the two users or a user and a service and saving the authentication session. The attacker can then replay the authentication session at a later time to gain access to resources or masquerade as a legitimate user. This may be possible with encrypted or clear-text protocols, depending on the controls implemented as part of the infrastructure. Replay attacks may also involve sending a duplicate transmission of data, resulting in data corruption or modification.

Command Injection

Command injection attacks allow attackers to use sessions that are already active for interaction with a service or an application. The premise of the attack may include injecting commands under the context of the application or service without the attacker authenticating first. This can be helpful to an attacker who wishes to inject data to a server or a client system when the session being hijacked has already undergone the initial authentication process.

Internet Control Message Protocol Redirect

Internet Control Message Protocol (ICMP) redirect attacks are another form of MITM attack. Some MITM tools will allow the attacker to create an ICMP redirect message (Type 5) to advertise that a better route is available for traffic traversing the network. An attacker can use this type of attack to force all traffic on the local area network through his or her computer. Once all data is traversing the attacker's computer, he or she may wish to sniff or modify it, depending on the goal of his or her attack.

Denial of Service

Denial-of-service (DoS) attacks can also be performed once an attacker has injected himself or herself between a victim and a remote resource. Attackers can route or drop traffic traversing his or her system to cause a DoS conditions. More information about DoS attacks is covered in Chapter 1, "Denial of Service."

DANGERS WITH MAN-IN-THE-MIDDLE ATTACKS

MITM attacks target users and systems by intercepting the data that flows between network endpoints. These attacks target not only the actual data that flows between endpoints but also the confidentiality and integrity of the data itself. When a user or a system falls prey to a MITM attack, all confidentiality of the communication should be considered lost. Since there is no more inherent trust between the endpoints of the communication, the confidentiality of the data can no longer be attested for.

Consider this example: Rob is sending instant messages to David using a plain text protocol. During the conversation, an attacker performs a MITM attack and starts eavesdropping on the conversation. During the conversation, Rob asks David to keep it a secret that he is meeting with an undercover agent, Alan, for lunch at a local Thai food restaurant. He also indicates that the meeting is private because they will be discussing recent reconnaissance operations conducted against potential threats to national security. Since our attacker has already performed a MITM attack, he or she knows the details of the meeting and all the confidentiality is now lost.

Continuing with the previous example, if the attacker were to modify the conversation between Rob and David, the integrity of the information passed between Rob and David would be lost. If the attacker changed the conversation outcome to invite David to the lunch meeting with the undercover agent, you could probably imagine the look of surprise on Rob and the undercover agent's face when David sits down and orders some Pad Thai. Some popular tools used for and during MITM attacks are listed in Table 6.1.

The following scenarios provide you with an overview of how some MITM attacks can be accomplished and introduce you to some of the tools used to facilitate MITM attacks.

Table 6.1 Man-in-the-middle tools

Cain	dsniff
Ettercap	Karma
AirJack	wsniff
Ucsniff	ARPoison
Wireshark	The Middler
SSLStrip	webmitm

Address Resolution Protocol Cache Poisoning

This first scenario describes the classic attack method of using Address Resolution Protocol (ARP) cache poisoning to inject an attacker in-between a user and the default gateway (router) to intercept and read data as it traverses the network. Before moving into the scenario, a quick refresher in ARP may help with your understanding of how this scenario is possible.

ARP (RFC 826[B]) is used in networks today to provide mapping of Open Systems Interconnection Reference Model (OSI) Layer 3 (Network) addresses to Layer 2 (Data Link) hardware addresses. Details and a good overview of the OSI model can be found at Cisco's Web site,[C] as well as in Chapter 5, "Spanning Tree Protocol." This mapping allows logical addresses, such as Internet Protocol (IP) addresses, to be associated with a physical hardware device such as a network interface card. Figure 6.2 provides an example of what an ARP table looks like when using the *arp –a* command from the Windows command prompt. Several different types of network implementations including Ethernet, Fast Ethernet, Fiber Distributed Data Interface, and wireless utilize ARP.

The following explanation assumes we are on a network using TCP/IP as the primary networking protocols. Communication using ARP is facilitated by the exchange of messages between hardware devices using ARP messages. The messages we are primarily concerned with are the *ARP request* and *ARP reply*. When requesting the hardware address of another system on the network, an ARP request is sent to the network *broadcast address* and includes the IP address and hardware address of the requestor and the IP address of the target system. Once a system receives the ARP request, it will check the local ARP table to see if it is the owner of the IP address broadcast in the original request. If the system does have an entry in its ARP table indicating it does own the IP address, an ARP reply is sent directly to the system that made the original request. The computer that made the original request will then add the hardware address to its ARP table for future use. A high-level overview of this operation is depicted in Figure 6.3.

The entire process of sending responses and receiving replies takes only seconds to complete in most cases, and this type of interaction is implemented on a variety of systems. ARP is used not only on computers but also on switches, routers, printers, wireless-enabled cell phones, and many other types of equipment.

[B]www.ietf.org/rfc/rfc826.txt

[C]www.cisco.com/en/US/docs/internetworking/technology/handbook/OSI-Protocols.html

```
C:\Windows\system32\cmd.exe                          _ □ ×

Interface: 192.168.1.196 --- 0xa
  Internet Address      Physical Address      Type
  192.168.1.1           00-06-b1-14-36-28     dynamic
  192.168.1.197         00-11-09-7f-5c-77     dynamic
  192.168.1.240         00-0d-9d-19-ef-13     dynamic
  192.168.1.245         00-21-29-eb-27-fb     dynamic
  192.168.1.255         ff-ff-ff-ff-ff-ff     static
  224.0.0.22            01-00-5e-00-00-16     static
  224.0.0.251           01-00-5e-00-00-fb     static
  224.0.0.252           01-00-5e-00-00-fc     static
  224.0.1.60            01-00-5e-00-01-3c     static
  239.255.255.250       01-00-5e-7f-ff-fa     static
  255.255.255.255       ff-ff-ff-ff-ff-ff     static
```

FIGURE 6.2

Windows XP ARP Table

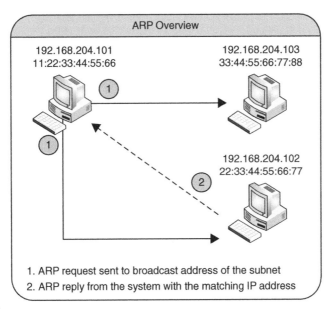

FIGURE 6.3

ARP Overview

Now that our refresher on ARP is complete, let's focus on a MITM attack using a technique referred to as ARP cache poisoning. The attacker wishes to perform a MITM attack in an effort to gain access to valid credentials that could allow him or her to interact with other network services. With the understanding of how ARP works and the availability of several common MITM tools, this attack is fairly easy to perform.

Several tools for performing ARP cache poisoning attacks are freely available via the Internet, and usage of the tools is usually well documented. The tool our attacker chooses for this scenario is Ettercap.[D] (See Chapter 7, "Password Replay" for an example of ARP poisoning using a different tool, Cain & Abel.) Some of the interesting features of this tool include host discovery, target selection interface, capability of performing several types of MITM attacks, sniffing, and a variety of plug-ins to use during attacks. The tool is also capable of being run on a several different computing platforms, and users have a choice of running the tool in a graphical user interface, ncurses,[E] or text-based environment.

TIP

The last paragraph explained the availability of tools and how well documented they are based on their popularity and developer documentation. Popular sites such as YouTube[F] allow people to create videos that will walk you through the common usage for many of the tools used for penetration testing and hacking. This is far from the days of reading text files and communicating on Bulletin Board Systems as a means of learning how to use and exchange tools. The learning curve today is significantly reduced for those getting started in security research and exploitation. Take a quick break, visit YouTube (or any other similar site), and search for "ettercap MITM." Also try searching for some of the tools or concepts we have discussed in this book.

The attacker in this scenario, Michael, works as a design engineer for a large company in the sleepy town of Seguin, Texas. The company sells and distributes a large product line of aftermarket motorcycle parts for those motorcycle enthusiasts who wish to add a little personality to their motorcycles. Recently, Michael was in an accident and had some extensive damage done to his personal motorcycle (although Michael was okay). It turns out the motorcycle was deemed a total loss by his insurance company and Michael ended up purchasing a new motorcycle. One thing that Michael dearly missed was his shiny and loud tailpipes; you could hear them coming from a mile away, and the tailpipes were the envy of everyone.

Being a team player, Michael decides to order replacement tailpipes for his new motorcycle from the company he works for so he can get back to cruising in style. However, he discovers the company has discontinued the model tailpipes he used to have and will not bring them back into production. This obviously makes Michael angry, and he decides to take some action to show the company what happens when they disrespect loyal employees and customers.

Since Michael has internal access to the network, he decides to use a MITM attack, so he can steal someone else's credentials to do some damage. Michael does this to reduce the likelihood the forthcoming attack will be traced back to him. Michael decides to use Ettercap to perform a MITM attack against Chip, the company

---

[D]http://ettercap.sourceforge.net/
[E]www.gnu.org/software/ncurses/ncurses.html
[F]www.youtube.com/

Web and database developer. Michael first scans the local network to obtain a list of IP addresses and host names on the network and is able to identify a Windows XP computer named *webdev* with an IP address of 192.168.204.139. The name of this computer sounds like it would be the one a Web developer may use so he takes note of the IP address and moves down his scan list. Michael also notices a Windows Server 2008 system named *corpweb* with an IP address of 192.168.204.131.

In an ARP cache poisoning attack, the attacker identifies two systems he wants to attack and then places himself in the middle of the communication stream. This is accomplished by using a tool such as Ettercap send false information to modify the ARP cache on the two target systems. The tool will send ARP packets to poison the ARP cache on the Windows 2008 Server indicating the MAC address of Chip's workstation is that of the attacker's computer. At the same time, ARP packets will be sent to poison the ARP cache on Chip's Windows XP computer to notify it the MAC address of the Windows 2008 Server is now that of the attacker's computer. Once the ARP cache poison completes, both of the victim systems will unknowingly route traffic intended for each other through the attacker computer. During this exchange of data, the Windows 2008 Server and the Windows XP computers both believe they are still directly communicating with each other.

Using Ettercap, the attacker is able to select the two systems identified previously and start an ARP cache poisoning attack against these systems. Upon successfully injecting himself or herself between Chip's computer and Web server, the attacker can sniff the traffic as it traverses his or her computer. Tools such as Ettercap have built-in filters to notify the attacker when credentials for specific protocols are sniffed during the attack. Figure 6.4 displays an active MITM attack as described in the scenario. It appears Michael was able to capture a File Transfer Protocol (FTP) login session originating from Chip's computer and authenticating to the Web server.

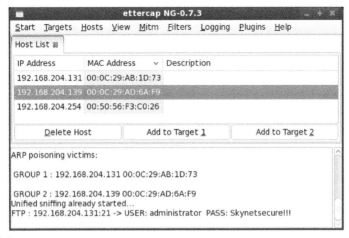

FIGURE 6.4

ARP MITM Password Capture

Since Michael knows that Chip is the company Web developer, there is a good chance that these credentials are used to upload Web site content and for routine access to the Web server and Web site files. Michael uses the login credentials against the FTP server and discovers not only that the credentials are valid but they place him in the root directory of the company Web site. With this type of access, Michael can possibly delete all the content, replace legitimate files, and browse for other credentials or important information on the server. Michael decides to upload an updated version of the main page of the Web site that reads "This week only, all parts are 50 percent off normal price!"

Obviously, the great deal on motorcycle parts being advertised on the Web site spreads fast and causes an increase in sales calls. After being tipped off by a customer that it is "great you're selling everything at half-off," the sales department goes into a panic. Selling most parts at 50 percent off normal price is costing the company money. What is a company to do? Honor the advertised special? Tell the customers there was a glitch and there is no sale? Tell the customers the site got hacked? You can draw your own conclusions, but the point is that a very simple attack can cause a company many messes to clean up.

Losing customer loyalty and tarnishing a good reputation can cause many companies to experience reduced revenue. In some cases, it can impact the company in such a way that it forces the company to reduce staff or even close their doors. Although this scenario was primarily about the execution of a MITM attack, any attacks with significant enough magnitude can really hurt the company overall.

Secure Sockets Layer Man-in-the-Middle

In the last scenario, we looked at the inner workings of how a typical ARP cache poison MITM attack works. Some of the tools used to perform these attacks are very powerful in themselves; however, with some additional tools, it is possible to increase the capabilities of the attacker. For instance, the last attack scenario allowed the attacker to obtain credentials sent to a FTP server. FTP provides no protection against sniffing attacks, which may expose credentials transmitted in clear text to an attacker using some of the techniques already discussed.

What about encrypted protocols such as SSL? By nature of its design, SSL is supposed to provide a layer of protection for those who wish to conduct transactions and log into services containing sensitive information. By using other tools such as *webmitm*[G] or *sslstrip*,[H] attackers can circumvent some SSL implementations to allow attackers to gain access to credentials and data that should have been protected from MITM attacks.

For this scenario, we observe our attacker as he uses a technique to obtain credentials from victims who believe they are accessing a secure SSL-enabled Web site. The attacker is at his or her local book store enjoying a large hazelnut coffee while

---

[G]www.monkey.org/~dugsong/dsniff/
[H]www.thoughtcrime.org/software/sslstrip/

finishing some research for one of his or her last classes for college. After a few hours of studying the inner workings of XML, he or she takes a break to clear his or her mind and observe some of the other coffee shop patrons.

Across from the attacker sits a man who appears to be very focused on finishing up some tasks on his work laptop. The attacker assumes it is a work laptop because of the sticker on the cover that makes it look like a work laptop—you know, the ones that say "PROPERTY of XYZ Company." This intrigues the attacker, so the attacker decides to perform a MITM attack to see what the man is up to. The attacker first identifies legitimate targets on a network by performing a discovery scan similar to the last scenario. During the scan, the attacker is most interested in identifying the victim computer and the default gateway.

After completing the scan, the attacker has identified the victim computer and the default gateway and can now prepare for his or her MITM attack. The attacker decides he or she is going to perform a SSL MITM attack to see if he or she can capture some credentials that the victim may be using. Specifically, the attacker will be using a tool called *sslstrip*.

The sslstrip tool created and supported by Moxie Marlinspike allows attackers to gain access to credentials transmitted using the HTTP and HTTPS protocols. The process includes setting up *iptables* to redirect all traffic sourced from the victim's computer to a predefined port running on the attacker's computer. The attacker then starts the sslstrip tool and performs an ARP MITM attack using tools such as arpspoof or Ettercap to inject himself or herself between the victim and the default gateway. At this point, sslstrip tracks the connections and listens for HTTP to HTTPS redirects to otherwise secure Web sites. When a victim attempts to log into a Web site using his or her credentials, sslstrip will write the username and password and the Web request to a log file for later viewing. The attacker can now reuse the captured credentials to access the victim's private data and quite possibly the data for the company the victim works for.

Now that we have an understanding of how sslstrip works, let's get back to the attack at hand. The commands in the following examples are executed on a Linux operating system with the appropriate Python[1] software installed. In the following command, the attacker creates a rule using iptables to accept all traffic from the victim's computer destined for TCP port 80 and redirect it to TCP port 10000 on the attacker's computer:

```
iptables -t nat -A PREROUTING -p tcp --destination-port 80
  -j REDIRECT --to-port 10000
```

Although the port used in this scenario is TCP port 10000, any available port can be used. Once the iptables rule is in place, the attacker can start the sslstrip tool and begin listening for inbound TCP traffic that was redirected from port 80 to port 10000, as seen in the next command:

```
./sslstrip.py --listen=10000
```

---

[1]www.python.org/

The final step of this attack involves using the arpspoof tool to perform a MITM cache poison attack against the victim's computer. In the following code example, arpspoof uses the attacker's eth0 network interface to perform the MITM attack between the target computer 192.168.204.139 and the default gateway address of 192.168.204.1:

```
arpspoof -i eth0 -10 192.168.204.139 192.168.204.1
```

After a few minutes of running the sslstrip tool, the attacker views the log files for the tool and can then use the credentials obtained to access accounts that would have been otherwise secure. The execution of this type of attack is fairly straightforward, and the consequences for falling victim to the attack can be disastrous, depending on the type of credentials obtained.

Domain Name System Spoofing

The final scenario we discuss in this chapter involves an attacker using the Domain Name System (DNS) to transmit false information about the true location of services requested by legitimate users. Before moving too far into how the attacker performs this type of attack, let's look at a high-level overview of what DNS does in normal operation.

When DNS is functioning normally, it answers requests of users who are trying to contact services by using domain names. For example, if a user wanted to go to the Microsoft Web site and see what new products are coming out soon, he or she would simply type www.microsoft.com into his or her Web browser. DNS would resolve the friendly and easy-to-remember address to its corresponding IP address. The browser would then direct the user to the IP address associated with www.microsoft.com, and the user can start browsing for the latest and greatest in Microsoft product offerings.

This DNS spoofing attack is performed by an attacker who runs an application capable of listening for and responding to DNS queries. One such tool is part of the dsniff suite of tools and is called *dnsspoof*. Once an attacker is running an application such as dnsspoof, he or she can listen for DNS requests that are sent from the DNS clients to a DNS server for resolution. Upon identifying a DNS request, the attacker can reply to the DNS client that made the request with an IP address for the requested domain. However, the attacker may decide to provide an IP address that is not really the address the DNS client was attempting to resolve.

As an example, if a user was attempting to connect to www.microsoft.com and an attacker was able to reply with the IP address of the fedoraproject.org Web site before a legitimate DNS server could reply, then the user would most likely redirected to the http://fedoraproject.org/ Web site instead of the site he or she intended on visiting.

Attackers can use techniques to redirect users to Web sites that appear safe but actually contain malicious code. In some cases, the attacker may create a Web site that looks almost identical to the real site and the user may never notice the difference. To put this into context, consider the scenario where you are going to visit online banking Web sites to check your account balance. An attacker performs a DNS spoofing attack to redirect you to a Web site that looks very similar to your online banking site. Upon visiting the Web site, you attempt to log into the Web site to check your account balance; however, after logging in the site displays a message indicating it is temporarily down for maintenance. Most people would not think anything of it and come back later to check their balance. However, the malicious Web site has already collected your username and password, and the attacker has already started selling your account information to other malicious people.

Although this technique varies quite a bit from the other two scenarios we already discussed, you can see how MITM attacks can be executed using a variety of methods. As time goes on, we find new methods are becoming more robust and deceptive as far as the capabilities of MITM attacks are concerned.

FUTURE OF MAN-IN-THE-MIDDLE ATTACKS

The future of MITM attacks is hard to predict; however, from the trend of attack development and research of similar attacks, it is expected to continue growing in scope. As recent as within the last year of the writing of this book (2010), presentations at network security conferences such as BlackHat[J] and DefCon[K] continue to highlight the importance and new developments of these types of attacks.

EPIC FAIL

One of the reasons network security initiatives and awareness fail is because administrators and designated security professionals are not provided proper funding for training to stay abreast of current threats. The threat landscape continues to evolve as can be witnessed by monitoring security-related Web sites, reading periodicals, and attending industry conferences.

As mentioned at the beginning of this section, many of the newest attacks and tools are released at security conferences such as BlackHat and DefCon every year. It is a wise investment to attend these conferences to really know what the threats are and witness the speed at which they are evolving.

Probably one of the most aggravating things to hear as a security professional is when administrators indicate they don't have time to stay up to date on the current threat landscape. Even better yet is sometimes hearing "we don't have any Internet facing services, so we are safe" from those who do not understand the threats. With proper training, with research, and by attending security-related conferences, the threat becomes more apparent.

Far too many times advice is given by security practitioners to make sure "end users are trained." However, it is just as important to ensure the people who are responsible for the overall network security posture are trained as well. Account for training and conference attendance into yearly budgets. Do it for the sake of your company's security preparation and awareness!

[J]www.blackhat.com/
[K]www.defcon.org/

Tools used to conduct these attacks continue to mature and are widely available to those who wish to use them. Several open-source projects continue to enhance their capabilities of making these attacks easy to conduct and provide attackers with a significant advantage. Thankfully we can help reduce the exploitable footprint of these types of attacks by implementing mitigating controls.

DEFENSES AGAINST MAN-IN-THE-MIDDLE ATTACKS

The previous examples have provided us with a pretty good overview of some of the dangers associated with MITM attacks. In this part of the chapter, we explore some of the possible countermeasures that can be deployed to help thwart MITM attacks and the impact they can have on your network. A few of the defensive considerations may allow for a stronger security posture for multiple parts of the overall network infrastructure, while others will focus specifically on defenses against MITM attacks.

Knowing the Threats

You have already taken the first step in securing your network by reading this chapter! Knowing the threats against your organization and how the threats can be identified and mitigated will provide the information you need to implement defensive controls. Whether the controls implemented are active controls to stop attacks in their tracks, or passive controls used to monitor for attacks, knowing the types of attacks used by attackers is one of the greatest things you can do to prepare.

Remember, the threat landscape is always changing, so a one-time investigation into the threats will only be a snapshot in time of what the threats are. Continued awareness of the threats and attack techniques will allow you to prepare defenses and stay vigilant in your defensive initiatives.

Defense-in-Depth Approach

The lack of defensive controls implemented on internal network segments is a primary reason many organizations fall victim to successful attacks. A prime example of this is the ability for an attacker to capture credentials and steal the network by way of MITM attacks. Implementing defensive security controls at various layers within the network allows for more challenges an attacker will have to overcome to be successful at obtaining his or her objective. This is often referred to as "defense-in-depth" by many security practitioners, and the notion of deploying defenses in this manner has been urged for many years. Protecting your perimeter assets is only a small part of a solid security plan.

Consider a real-world example of defense-in-depth: when planning military operations, it is common for leaders to deploy defensive measures to deter successful attacks on military installations, equipment, and personnel. For instance, let's explore the defensive posture for an US Army Airborne Infantry unit protecting a command and control outpost. For a first line of defense, the infantry unit will most likely have several Observation Point/Listening Points forward of the main defensive positions to give early warning of pending attacks. Additionally, early warning devices that trigger flares and noisemaking devices can also alert units to possible threats. In the information security world, these would be similar to the capabilities Intrusion Detection Systems (IDSes) provide. Early detection is vital to minimizing the impact of attacks, reducing potential losses.

A secondary defensive measure for protecting the command post would be using physical barriers to impede swift movement of the enemy. These barriers can be landscape and terrain that form a nature barrier such as a hill or trench. In information security, they may be equivalent to a well-placed proxy or firewall device. The goal of this line of defense is to slow attacks or at least to make it very tedious to perform them.

Next we look at defenses that are a little closer to the command and control point. These would be razor wire, mines, and small-caliber weapons. (Although there are other layers of defense as far as military strategy is concerned, the goal of this example is to provide a general overview of strategies, not to make us all hardened military warriors.) These controls provide the last line of defense for the soldiers. In a networking environment, these can equate to desktop security such as malware and virus protection, host-based firewalls and IDS, patch management, and system auditing controls.

Implementing some of these controls will reduce the overall likelihood of an attacker being successful in his or her attacks. But just as a soldier needs to be fed, rested, and outfitted with the correct equipment, your network should also ensure that it is constantly being monitored for its health and well-being. Why is this important? Because you cannot go down to your local network equipment vendor to purchase a single product that will satisfy *all* the needs of your network security program. Security is a process, not a product, and each layer provides a part of the overall solution. Now that we have explored an overview of defense in depth, we can focus our attention to specific defenses for MITM attacks.

Public Key Infrastructure

One possible solution to address MITM attacks involves deploying a Public Key Infrastructure (PKI) that implements mutual authentication. PKI manages the use of public key cryptography as we know it today. Think of it as the system that is responsible for the "care and feeding" of public key cryptography. In a PKI, there are several components that handle the issuance and revocation of certificates as well as attesting for the validity of certificates that are implemented. These are important components as it is the basis of ensuring we can trust encryption, signatures, and the implementation a given PKI is responsible for.

As it relates to SSL and HTTPS connections, the process used to verify the validity of a certificate is as follows: when connecting to a server that is using a digitally signed SSL certificate, the server will send the certificate to the Web user's browser. Upon verification of the validity of the SSL certificate, the browser will connect to the server using the SSL protocol. A session key is created and used to protect the data that travels between the user's browser and the server. The session key is unique to the session and is used as a means of ensuring private communication between the user and the Web server.

> **WARNING**
>
> Implementing a PKI by itself is not enough to prevent MITM attacks. If an attacker can capture key exchanges at the beginning of a session, he or she may still be able to perform MITM attacks. For this reason, implementing other controls that complement PKI implementations should be considered.

Although PKI on its own is not a sufficient mitigating control against MITM attacks, when it is coupled with mutual authentication, the solution is more appealing. Mutual authentication is the concept of requiring not just a client to authenticate to a server but also the server to authenticate to the client. With many client and server implementations, the initial trust is only confirmed by a one-way verification between the client and the server. With mutual authentication, the server verifies the client and the client verifies the server to ensure legitimate communications are being exchanged. Verification can be conducted by using public and private keys.

As with many security control implementations, there may be additional costs with the configuration of PKI and mutual authentication. The overall solution provides a decent return on investment as far as defending against MITM attacks is concerned. Implementing mutual authentication and PKI together can increase the complexity of and significantly reduce the likelihood of successful MITM attacks.

Port Security

Many organizations do not take into account what access the public may have to the network infrastructure when designing the physical layout of the network access points and the location of network jacks. One of the dangers associated with deploying a network is that, in many cases, anyone who can access a network jack can connect to and access network resources. Although this concept may not be apparent to many, it is indeed a very real threat. Even in trusted areas, security can be compromised by allowing access to visitors who may require temporary Internet access.

Port security allows administrators to lock down some of the loose ends that may be left exposed to some of the threats we have discussed in this chapter. In addition to being able to restrict the access of unauthorized systems, the implementation of port security can also reduce the organization's exposure to the MITM attacks. Several vendors offer products that allow network integrators to implement port security, including Cisco,[L] Juniper,[M] and HP.[N]

[L] www.cisco.com/
[M] www.juniper.net
[N] www.hp.com/

Port security allows administrators to assign rules to access interfaces to determine if devices connecting to ports are indeed authorized to connect and access the network. This type of filtering can be accomplished by the administrator configuring switches on a port-by-port basis manually or dynamically by switch software. Once configured correctly, the switch can identify suspicious network traffic and devices that may not be authorized to connect to the network and immediately restrict traffic while also notifying administrators of potential security issues.

Some implementations of port security will determine access based on what hardware addresses are connected to each port. For example, in a situation where port security is enabled and a desktop computer is plugged into the switch port, the switch will learn the physical address of the desktop computer and only allow that hardware device to connect on that port. Should someone disconnect the desktop computer and attempt to plug in a laptop or other device, the port would identify the change and shut down the port. Once again, a notification may be sent to administrators to warn of potential issues. Although this sounds like a logical method of restricting access, if an attacker has the physical address of the initial device connected to the port he or she may be able to spoof the physical address to gain access via the port.

Some devices have the capability of implementing dynamic ARP inspection as a method of detecting gratuitous ARP replies and preventing them from being relayed. This is accomplished by the device having the capability of determining what ARP traffic is allowed.

Use Encrypted Protocols

Although the threat of sniffing and MITM attacks has been around for some time, many organizations fail to implement the best security practices to help reduce the overall exposure of an organization to these types of attacks. Organizations should implement encrypted protocols whenever possible to reduce the likelihood credentials will be sniffed off the network by attackers.

Some examples of clear-text protocols still heavily used in networks today include FTP, TELNET, and HTTP. Most clear-text protocols today have an encrypted alternative that can provide an additional layer of security. Some of the popular alternatives for the previously mentioned protocols include SFTP, SSH, and HTTPS. It is important to keep in mind that encrypted protocols should be used for protecting communications for remote administration and for protecting sensitive data that is being transmitted for everyday applications.

Implementing encrypted protocols not only protects data while it is in transit but also can add an additional layer of complexity for attackers to deal with when trying to perform attacks such as an MITM attack. As a basic security recommendation, encrypted protocols should always be used instead of clear-text protocols, not just because of the threat of MITM attacks, but for the protection of data while in transit in general.

Low-Level Detection

Implementing controls at various points in the network will ultimately provide a good defensive strategy. However, looking at some of the low-level detection methods will also pay off. A few simple things you can do if you suspect MITM attacks are being performed include reviewing local ARP table information and network traffic.

Although the intent is to use a more centralized and robust method of viewing the health of the network as a whole, a simple test you can perform to see if you are currently being attacked is to review ARP table entries. Figure 6.5 illustrates the ARP table for a Windows XP that is currently a victim of an ARP cache poison attack. This screenshot was actually taken from the victim computer in the lab environment while preparing for the section "ARP Cache Poisoning."

After reviewing Figure 6.5, we can see that multiple IP addresses appear to have the same physical address. This means that the computer with IP address 192.168.204.139 has ARP table entries indicating both 192.168.204.1 and 192.168.204.131 reside at the same physical location. In this case, 192.168.204.1 is the IP address of the attacker's computer and 192.168.204.131 is actually a Windows 2008 Domain Controller. If you detect something similar to this on your network, you should conduct further investigation to find out the source of the issue.

As you may recall from the section "ARP Cache Poisoning," devices broadcast ARP requests to the broadcast address of the network in an effort to locate other systems on the network. During an active ARP cache poisoning attack, multiple IP addresses will have the same hardware address, as explained in the last paragraph. Figure 6.6 displays what an administrator may see while sniffing the network during such an attack.

Tools such as Wireshark will usually provide immediate identification of multiple devices using the same hardware address. Figure 6.6 is an example of a capture performed while performing a MITM attack on a network where the attacker

FIGURE 6.5

Detecting ARP MITM

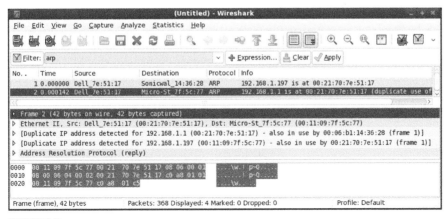

FIGURE 6.6

Protocol Detection of ARP MITM

was injecting himself or herself between a Windows XP computer (192.168.1.197) and the router interface for the subnet (192.168.1.1). The hardware address of 00:21:70:7E:51:17 is actually the address of the attacker's computer.

One example of a network-based tool for monitoring the status of IP address to hardware address mapping is *Arpwatch*.[O] Arpwatch is an application developed several years ago by the Network Research Group at Lawrence Berkeley National Laboratory.[P] This tool monitors network traffic and builds a database of hardware-to-IP address relationships and time-stamps them to indicate when they were added to the database. The application has the ability to notify administrators via e-mail or syslog messages of changes to the hardware to IP address mapping. Changes may indicate MITM attacks are being performed. Although this tool is several years old, many applications used to monitor malicious traffic today still follow similar concepts.

SUMMARY

This chapter provided an overview, examples, and several defensive considerations for MITM attacks. The overview of MITM attacks provided valuable information about how the attacks work and how they can be performed using various methods of attack. This allows administrators and those responsible for security within their organizations to understand the threats that face the organization.

The examples of these types of attacks paint a picture of what a few scenarios for using MITM may look like and how various methods of attack can be used by an attacker in different situations. Although several scenarios were discussed and

---

[O]ftp://ftp.ee.lbl.gov/arpwatch.tar.gz
[P]http://ee.lbl.gov/

explained, it is important to stay abreast of new developments in MITM attack methods by following network security news sources.

The final portion of this chapter provided several options for administrators to consider when implementing controls to help reduce the likelihood of MITM attacks. Using defense-in-depth to protect the network at various levels was reviewed along with several recommendations for protecting against threats associated specifically with MITM attacks.

Password Replay

INFORMATION IN THIS CHAPTER

- How Password Replay Works
- Dangers of Password Replay
- Defending against Password Replay
- The Future of Password Replay

It seems that in 2003 (although the exact year differs in different accounts) hackers aimed an antenna at a Marshalls clothing store near St. Paul, Minnesota, in order to capture data from the store's wireless network. By capturing network traffic and analyzing it, the hackers were able to obtain the wireless network password. Once they were in, they were able to "sniff" for other passwords on the network, eventually obtaining access to the databases of parent company TJX in Framingham, Massachusetts. Ultimately, the hackers downloaded around 94 million credit card numbers.[A] They also got personal information, including Social Security numbers, for about 451,000 customers. TJX personnel discovered the intrusion in December 2006, and found files left behind by the hackers. Perhaps ironically, TJX cannot break the encryption the hackers used on the files. The cost for TJX? Aside from significant embarrassment the total cost could top $1 billion over 5 years to pay for security consultants, lawyers, and of course marketing to help reassure customers. Of course, this figure does *not* include potential liabilities from lawsuits.[B] Who will sue? Affected banks, for one, are alleging negligence in TJX security practices. There's also the Federal Trade Commission (FTC). Sometimes life is tough.

Much of this intrusion was accomplished using the technique of *password replay*. The security used on the wireless network, wired equivalent privacy (WEP), was

---

[A]For the 94 million figure, see Ross Kerber, "Court Filing In TJX Breach Doubles Toll," *Boston Globe*, October 24, 2007.
[B]There are many articles on the TJX break-in. In particular, see "How Credit-Card Data Went Out Wireless Door," *The Wall Street Journal*, May 4, 2007.

cracked using a variant of password replay, and then passwords were captured from the unencrypted network traffic. This allowed the intruders to make their way along the TJX networks and copy out the contents of databases. Even better, they were able to install software at points in the network to "sniff" the unencrypted credit card data traveling the network.

Of course this was all years ago. On January 20, 2009, Heartland Payment Systems (HPS) announced a bigger breach. HPS employees discovered programs on their network to capture traffic. In this case, the thieves compromised an estimated 100 million credit cards. This information isn't just the credit card numbers, but includes the full data in the magnetic stripe of the card, allowing the thieves easily to create duplicate cards.[C]

The good news? It looks like the mastermind of both operations has been caught. Albert Gonzalez has pleaded guilty.[D] He leaves behind a record of computer break-ins and $1.1 million in cash discovered wrapped in plastic and buried in a drum in his parents' backyard.[E] Again, sometimes life is tough.

HOW PASSWORD REPLAY WORKS

It's 1995, and you're sitting in your office arguing in an online newsgroup about the new show *Star Trek: Voyager*. Your "friend" Rob stops by and you chat for a while. Before he leaves Rob asks if he can use your terminal to check his e-mail. "Sure," you tell him. Rob logs in, checks his e-mail, and the logs out. Or so it seems.

After Rob leaves you decide to log in and check out this new online bookstore you've heard about. You log in, and you are told your password is incorrect. You've mistyped it before, so you type it again, and it is accepted. After visiting the bookstore's Web site you decide "Hmph. You can't actually flip through the books, and the Web is too insecure. This will never catch on."

Not only are you wrong about the bookstore but also Rob now has your password. You've just been the victim of a fake login that allowed Rob to capture your password. It's shockingly easy to do this in most cases. For example, if you are using Ubuntu 9.10 and use console login instead of the graphical login, then the script shown in Figure 7.1 will emulate the log-in prompt, capture the next username and password, report that the password is in error, and then terminate itself. The end result looks just as it should. People happily accept that they have mistyped their password once, and so no suspicion is aroused.

You'd log in on the first text console (named "tty1") and run this script. The effect is as if you had logged out; but of course, you haven't. The script prints an official-looking

---

[C]Rachael King, "Lessons From the Data Breach at Heartland," *BusinessWeek*, July 6, 2009.

[D]"Man Accused of Stealing Stores' Data Pleads Guilty," (REUTERS), *The New York Times*, August 28, 2009.

[E]Scott Hiaasen, Rob Barry, Nirvi Shah, and Michael Sallah, "From Snitch to Cyberthief of the Century," *The Miami Herald*, August 22, 2009.

```
#!/bin/bash
clear
echo ""
while [ -z $login ] ; do
   echo "Ubuntu 9.10 ubuntu tty1"
   echo ""
   read -p "ubuntu login: " login
done
stty -echo
read -p "Password: " password
stty echo
echo ""
echo "Login incorrect"
echo "$login:$password" > capture.log
kill  -9 $PPID $$ >/dev/null
```

FIGURE 7.1

A Very Simple Fake Login

log-in prompt and captures the username and password (character echo is turned off for the password so that things appear correct). The script then claims you have entered the wrong credentials, saves what you *did* enter, and kills itself and your log-in shell. Presto! You're logged out and the data is captured. Your victim now gets a *real* log-in prompt and can log in.

University computer labs used to be (and some still are) full of UNIX workstations with console logins, and this was a not-too-uncommon occurrence. There are advantages to having a login that is not your own, especially if you are planning to do something dastardly. System administrators would sometimes watch

---

NOTE

You don't use a console UNIX login, so you're golden, right? Well, no. Graphical user interface logins can be spoofed as well, and it is both easy and effective. Just write a program that uses the whole screen to display the appropriate login, and then capture the data entered. On some systems, you can use this information to actually log the person in, so when they log out your "fake" login is ready to accept the next victim.

Microsoft has addressed this in more recent versions of Windows by requiring the user to press **Ctrl + Alt + Del** to initiate a login. This is a good idea, as this key combination cannot be trapped by the fake login. Or can it?

There are actually several approaches to trapping the **Ctrl + Alt + Del** combination that work just fine. After all, this is often done for "kiosk" installations of Windows, where a single application has to be running all the time, no matter what. These require that the computer user has administrative access to the operating system, so he or she can modify the keyboard driver, modify the registry, or (for versions earlier to Vista) manipulate the graphical identification and authentication (GINA) library. There's an open source implementation of GINA for you to start your hacking: pGINA.[F]

[F]See http://sourceforge.net/projects/pgina/.

for unoccupied machines with someone still logged in; it could be someone who forgot to log out, or something more nefarious. The "solution" to these watchful eyes is trivial social engineering: wait until the lab is full, start the program, and then kindly hand off the terminal to the next person who is waiting. The script logs you out and then the other person logs in; everything is just as it should be. Well, mostly.

Although this isn't an example of a *network* attack, it illustrates an important point about security. Passwords are typically *static* and *trusted*. That is, they don't change (at least, not very often), and they often serve as a single point of authentication that you are who you say you are. They are similar to physical keys or proximity cards ("prox cards" or "key cards") in this regard. If you have the key or the proximity card (or a duplicate), you have access.

The important distinction between passwords and physical keys or proximity cards is that the latter is intended to prevent physical trespass; you have to go to the location, and there may be guards who do not recognize your face, cameras to take your picture, and suspicious employees. You probably have to get dressed. Life is sometimes tough. Passwords prevent *virtual* trespass, and you may be able to accomplish this from the (relative) comfort of your parent's basement while wearing your bathrobe. Another important distinction is that the information you really, really want is likely stored on computers, anyway. Why get off the couch if you don't have to?

WARNING

Fake logins are *very* common on the Internet.[G] *Phishing* is a very common attack that combines social engineering with password capture to steal log-in credentials, credit card numbers, or other personal information. Most phishing e-mails direct you to a Web site purporting to be your bank, credit card company, or employer. When you enter your credentials or other information on the site, however, it is captured and saved. You may then be directed to the real site.

The best way to detect this sort of attempt is to carefully examine the Web address (URL) in the message and see if it is really the site you expect. The best way to avoid phishing scams is to simply *never click on a link in an e-mail* unless it is from someone you trust or in a communication you are expecting (such as a registration confirmation e-mail). Even then you should examine the link; it is possible that a "man in the middle" (see Chapter 6, "Man-in-the-Middle") could rewrite the link to point to their site. Legitimate organizations should never send you e-mail with instruction to click a link and enter personally identifiable information. If you need to log in to your bank, enter your bank's address or use a bookmark, and then log in.

[G]A fake Google mail (Gmail) login is described at http://www.trap17.com/index.php/fake-gmail-interface_t57079.html (retrieved on December 1st, 2009). The interesting thing about this fake login is just how similar it is to the UNIX command-line attack described previously in this section. After the fake login captures your credentials, it forwards you to the *real* Gmail site. Note that the fake login has long since been taken down.

Simple Password Sniffing

One way to capture passwords on a network is to capture and decode network packets. As discussed in Chapter 5, "Spanning Tree Attacks," Wireshark,[H] tcpdump, and libpcap[I] can be used to capture packets. If you have access to a node through which the packets will travel, and the passwords are unencrypted, you can capture them very easily. Note that this is a form of the "man in the middle" attack detailed in Chapter 6, "Man-in-the-Middle."

This method of password capture assumes two things are happening.

1. Static password authentication is required.
2. Passwords are being sent as "clear text," that is, unencrypted.

Surely nobody would do this, you might say. Well, they do. For example, this might be done if the communication channel is itself encrypted, as with a virtual private network (VPN). This works great to secure traffic between your machine and a remote network; traffic passing through intermediate nodes is encrypted. It does not work so well if someone has access to the remote network or, in some cases, to your machine. Once someone breaks into the remote network by some means (see the

---

> **NOTE**
>
> What's your password policy? There are approximately 95 characters that are typically usable in passwords. Letting a user choose *any* password gives a grand total of more than six *quadrillion* possible passwords of length up to eight. That's actually a lot, and includes such gems as "password" and "O),,!*fZ".
>
> We believe (with good reason) that the password "O),,!*fZ" is harder to crack than "password" because many password-cracking tools use dictionary-based attacks, and so we establish rules to promote stronger passwords. We might require at least one digit, at least one lower- and one upper-case letter, and at least one nonalphanumeric character. This limits our choice on four characters, and restricts the realm of possible eight-character or shorter passwords to roughly 18 *trillion*. That's much, much fewer, and is pushing us into the realm of effective brute-force attacks. In fact, it becomes possible to precompute tables that can instantly crack any such password.
>
> This is a tension between usability and security. Is the password "O),,!*fZ" better than, say, "hgqpmngd"? Well, keep in mind that some password-cracking tools such as Cain & Abel,[J] described in the later section "Password Replay," explicitly include code to run a brute-force attack on lower-case-only passwords. It is, of course, possible to go completely wrong with your policy. The more restrictive you make your policy, the smaller the search space for an attacker.
>
> Requiring your users to change their passwords periodically and to avoid reuse of old passwords can be a good policy. They are less likely to change their passwords everywhere else, so it is highly unlikely that their account on your enterprise resource planning (ERP) system and their account on startrek.com share the same password. That's a good thing.

[H]See http://www.wireshark.org/. Note that this tool was previously named Ethereal.
[I]See http://www.tcpdump.org/ for tcpdump (a command line tool) and libpcap (a library).
[J]See http://www.oxid.it/cain.html. Users of non-Windows operating systems should have a look at dsniff: http://www.monkey.org/~dugsong/dsniff/.

rest of this book) then they can sniff packets and look for clear text passwords. This gives them access to other accounts, possibly to other data, and perhaps even to your accounts on *other* networks. Do you use different passwords for all your accounts? Do you ever reuse old passwords? If somebody has a list of the passwords you used last year they can use these to start guessing your current passwords.

Running a tool like Wireshark on a network node and watching for Post Office Protocol (POP) or Simple Mail Transfer Protocol (SMTP) traffic[K] can often reveal interesting data. Of course, combing through all the captured traffic can be burdensome. Can't someone automate that task for us? Of course they can. EffeTech makes a commercial password sniffer called Ace Password Sniffer,[L] and NirSoft SniffPass[M] is a freeware utility that captures packets and watches for passwords in commonly used protocols. These are just two; a quick Web search for "password sniffer" can turn up many, many more. These are typically advertised as a way to recover lost passwords or monitor children on the Internet, but as with most tools, they have other uses.

> **WARNING**
>
> Suppose you're running Wireshark. You may be trying to capture packets in an attempt to break into a machine, but more likely you are a network administrator trying to monitor your network. Wireshark has to read and respond to essentially arbitrary data, and typically does so while running as the "root" administrative user (so it can capture all traffic). Security vulnerabilities in Wireshark, or any other such program, can actually lead to an attacker gaining control of the machine where Wireshark is running! Keep your software up-to-date and pay attention to suggestions for securely running software like Wireshark that needs special privileges.

All these depend on your ability to "sniff" the traffic. That is, the traffic has to pass through (or be available to) your machine. There are a variety of ways to get the traffic. The most straightforward is just to install the password sniffer (or a traffic-capture program like tcpdump) on a gateway or proxy server. You can then watch all the traffic passing through the machine on its way to and from the Internet. It may even be possible to modify a network's topology (see Chapter 5, "Spanning Tree Attacks") so that your machine receives all traffic. You can only sift through the traffic you actually see, after all.

Of course, sometimes people decide to broadcast all their packets to the world. The mechanism to accomplish this heightened level of insecurity is called "wireless networking," and you can often find unencrypted wireless networks in coffee and sandwich shops. Although you might not be able to break into some well-secured corporate network, you might discover that the vice-president has an unsecured (or poorly secured) wireless network at home, and he tends to use the same passwords

---

[K]POP is a very common protocol for mail delivery (getting the mail from the server to you), while SMTP is a very common protocol for sending mail (getting the mail from you to the server).
[L]See http://www.effetech.com/aps/.
[M]See http://www.nirsoft.net/utils/password_sniffer.html.

for everything, from his corporate e-mail to protecting his VPN certificates. Using his e-mail account, you might even compose angry e-mails "from him" to the corporate IT department. Who knows what you might accomplish this way?

Password Replay

You've got the access to a switch that is carrying your "friend" Rob's Internet traffic, and you are happily collecting packets. You see that he occasionally connects to a remote site and you are *sure* he is busy extolling the virtues of Kirk as captain of the *Enterprise* and running down your recent postings about Picard. You have to know for sure, but you can't capture any clear-text passwords. The system he is using encrypts his credentials when he sends them, so you can't just grab them from the network traffic. What can you do?

You may be able to *replay* the packets. Replay attacks work by first recording an authentication session, and then playing that session back at a later time. Using this strategy you may be able to observe Rob's authentication session, and then replay the recorded packets at a later time to gain access as if you were Rob.

Recording and playing back packets sounds like something that requires programming. Luckily there are ready-made tools such as tcpreplay[N] to automate most of this process for you. Actually, "tcpreplay" is a suite of tools for classifying, editing, and replaying network traffic. These tools work from a "pcap" file containing captured traffic, created with another tool like tcpdump. The tools are quite sophisticated.

"Sophisticated" might sound like another word for "hard to use." All you want to do is get Rob's password. Do you really have to capture traffic, sift through it to find the kind of packets you want, extract those (you can use tcpdump to refilter an existing pcap file), classify the packets so you get the client (Rob's) traffic, edit the traffic if necessary to modify the IP addresses, and then replay the traffic? Whew! Stealing—I mean, "recovering" passwords from network traffic must be a common activity. Isn't there an easier way?

Of course there is. One of the best tools around for this sort of work is a freeware tool called Cain & Abel. This is one of those cases where Windows users have an exceptionally powerful tool that really isn't available for other operating systems. After you've downloaded and installed Cain & Abel (but see the TIP box first!) you are ready to begin capturing passwords, conversations, and other network traffic.

Replay is another exploitation of a static (or at least predictable) authentication system. If the challenge and response depend on a sequence number that is not predictable by the eavesdropper, then password replay will probably fail. In fact, including a cryptographic sequence number is the most common means to prevent password replay attacks. Given this, you might think that practical password replay is a nonstarter—but you'd be wrong. Many systems are susceptible to replay attacks. You may have some of these systems in your infrastructure right now.

[N]See http://tcpreplay.synfin.net/trac/.

> **TIP**
>
> Cain & Abel is a well-known password sniffer. In fact, it is so well known – and so effective – that antivirus and antimalware vendors detect it. You may not be able to install it if you have an active antivirus program on your machine running in an "auto protect" mode. Antivirus scans might discover the program and damage or remove it by trying to "quarantine" parts of it. They may either prevent the "Abel" service from starting, or detect and kill it. How rude! All you want to do is capture passwords. What's so wrong about that? The lesson is that you should disable your antivirus software before you download, install, and run Cain & Abel.
>
> The Cain & Abel software expects to be able to intercept packets. An active firewall's rules can interfere with some aspects of the program, so you might want to also disable the firewall before you run the program. Disabling the antivirus and the firewall on a machine can be dangerous—but Rob should have thought about that before he started rambling on about *Star Trek*, something he clearly knows nothing about. It's his own fault, really, that you had to install a password sniffer on his machine.
>
> Installation of Cain & Abel requires reading the instructions; you have to install and start the Abel service separately from the Cain front end. There is also a method to remotely install the Abel service and start it on another machine, and then connect to it with the Cain interface.
>
> If you install Cain & Abel on a machine used by others, they may detect it. By default Cain & Abel installs the registry key HKEY_CURRENT_USER\Software\Cain. In short, the program is fairly easy to detect, and isn't really intended to be hidden. Perhaps after you are done using it, you may consider running the uninstaller that comes with it. It is, after all, courteous to clean up after yourself.

What about encrypted traffic and passwords, or protocols using sequence numbers? It might be surprising to know that these can also fall prey to replay attacks for several reasons:

- The protocol might be cryptographically weak.
- The protocol might have a fundamental weakness that exposes credentials.
- It may be possible to use a man-in-the-middle attack to overcome the encryption.

An example of a cryptographically weak protocol is WEP,[O] a protocol used to secure wireless networks. Sadly, the protocol is constructed in such a manner that it is possible to quickly break the encryption by capturing special packets called *initialization vectors* (IV). This attack was used in the TJX break-in described at the start of this chapter.[P] Several tools exist that can be used to sniff packets, collect IVs, and then crack the wireless password. Because it can take a while to collect enough packets, these tools commonly support packet *injection*, where the attacking machine generates traffic to cause the wireless hub to generate new IVs. The Aircrack-ng tools[Q] provides wireless network cracking under Windows and Linux for WEP, as well as

---

[O]See IEEE standard 802.11-1997.
[P]See Larry Greenemeier, "T.J. Maxx Data Theft Likely Due to Wireless 'Wardriving,'" EE Times, May 9th, 2007. http://www.eetimes.com/.
[Q]See http://www.aircrack-ng.org/.

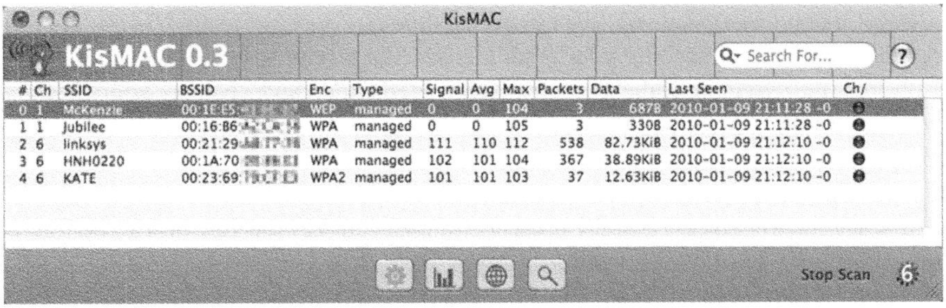

FIGURE 7.2

KisMAC

the more modern wi-fi protected access (WPA). Mac users have the KisMAC tool.[R] Figure 7.2 shows KisMAC running and collecting packets for several networks. Once enough packets have been captured, the cleartext WEP password can be cracked.

Server Message Block (SMB) is a protocol for network communication between network nodes and to shared devices such as printers. SMB is the application-layer network protocol of the Microsoft Windows network and is used throughout the Windows world. NT LAN Manager (NTLM) is an authentication protocol used with SMB in Windows versions earlier to Vista. (It is still present in Vista, but deprecated. Kerberos[S] is the new authentication system.) There is a chance that, at the time of writing, your infrastructure may still be using a version of this authentication protocol with a fundamental weakness: it honors remote requests for authentication. Suppose you receive an e-mail from your "friend" Rob inviting you to join a Kirk vs. Picard discussion, and providing you a link. You immediately click on the link to give everyone the benefit of your opinion. When you click the link, you are connected to

---

EPIC FAIL

SMB has been known to be "broken" since 2001, but changing a network protocol is a nontrivial matter. Lots of devices and network-based applications depend on the protocol implementation, and changing them all at once isn't really an option. You don't want your e-mail to quit working, do you? Microsoft kept working on a way to fix the problem, eventually releasing patch MS08-068[T] in November 2008. So you only had 7 years to exploit this particular vulnerability. Of course, it took until July 2007 to implement the exploit in the Metasploit 3 framework.[U] At the time of writing, there are other outstanding security issues that Microsoft is currently working on. As you read this, that is probably still true.

[R]See http://kismac-ng.org/.
[S]Kerberos is a very common authentication protocol under Windows, Linux, and UNIX, including OS X. See http://web.mit.edu/Kerberos/.
[T]See http://www.microsoft.com/technet/security/Bulletin/MS08-068.mspx.
[U]See http://www.metasploit.com/. Metasploit was created in 2003, so it only took four years to get around to writing that particular exploit.

a server that requests that you (the client) authenticate yourself using NTLM. NTLM responds by happily sending your credentials to the server, which stores them. Later Rob logs into your machine with the stolen credentials and changes your desktop wallpaper to an image of Picard and even goes so far as to delete your fan script. People can be so mean.

Finally, it is possible to use a variant of the man-in-the-middle attack to capture and replay passwords even in the presence of encryption. Precisely how to do that is the subject of the following section.

Address Resolution Protocol Poison Routing

In Figure 7.3, Alice wants to connect to the server out on the Internet. Her traffic flows through the gateway, to which Eve is also connected. We see the Internet Protocol (IP) and media access control (MAC) addresses for the machines. Chapter 5, "Spanning Tree Attacks," discusses exploiting the Spanning Tree Protocol, a "layer 2" protocol. Another layer 2 protocol is the Address Resolution Protocol (ARP). ARP is used to map between IP addresses and MAC addresses. Although a network card might be assigned any of several IP addresses over the course of its life, it (typically) has a single permanent MAC address.[V]

Alice wants to communicate with the server, but it is on a different network. She therefore sends her traffic to the gateway with IP 10.1.2.1. Her machine's

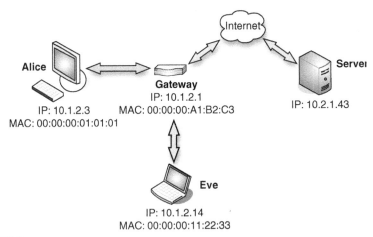

FIGURE 7.3

Preparing to Eavesdrop

[V]Of course, "permanent" here takes on its computer science meaning of "not really permanent." That is, it is possible to assign the card a different MAC address. This is called MAC "spoofing," and it has a variety of benevolent and malevolent uses.

ARP tables indicate that this IP address belongs to the machine with MAC address 00:00:00:A1:B2:C3. The gateway then takes care of forwarding the traffic on to the Internet. Likewise, packets arriving at the gateway for Alice's machine are mapped to MAC address 00:00:00:01:01:01.

Eve wants to listen to the traffic between Alice and the server (or between Alice and the whole Internet, for that matter). To accomplish this, Eve uses ARP "poisoning," sometimes (confusingly) referred to by the acronym APR for ARP poison routing. Eve sends out an ARP update to Alice's machine at 00:00:00:01:01:01 pointing the IP address 10.1.2.1 to Eve's MAC address 00:00:00:11:22:33, and Alice's machine dutifully stores this in its cache. Eve then sends out an ARP update to the gateway machine at 00:00:00:A1:B2:C3 pointing the IP address 10.1.2.3 to Eve's MAC address 00:00:00:11:22:33. Eve's machine can still route traffic to the gateway and to Alice's machine using the correct MAC addresses. Now Alice's machine thinks Eve's machine is the router, and the router thinks Eve's machine is Alice's.

Alice wants to log into the server, so she sends a request to the server. The server is on a different network, so her machine determines that it needs to be sent to the gateway at IP 10.1.2.1. Alice's machine looks in the ARP cache and finds MAC address 00:00:00:11:22:33, and sends the packets to that MAC address. In this case, the gateway is connected to Eve's machine, but the packets are labeled for 00:00:00:11:22:33, so the gateway sends them on to Eve's machine. Eve can now modify the packets however she wants and then send them to the gateway at MAC address 00:00:00:A1:B2:C3. The gateway is the destination for these packets, so it examines them, and determines whether they should be sent on to the Internet.

Next the server replies to Alice. Packets arrive at the gateway destined for IP address 10.1.2.3. The gateway looks in its ARP cache and determines that this IP address belongs to the machine with MAC address 00:00:00:11:22:33. It then sends the packets on to Eve's machine. Eve is now free to modify the packets however she wishes, and then she sends the modified packets on to MAC address 00:00:00:01:01:01. The gateway receives these packets that are not for it, and dutifully forwards them on to Alice's machine. Eve has successfully become the (wo)man in the middle.

Now, Alice wants to establish a secure communications channel, say with hypertext transfer protocol secure (HTTPS). The following things would typically happen:

1. Alice creates an HTTPS request and sends it to the remote server.
2. The server responds, identifying itself with a cryptographic certificate.
3. Alice's browser checks that the certificate (a) is valid for the original Web address, and (b) has a chain of trust to some well-known and trusted third party, whose public certificate is stored in the browser.
4. Alice and the server are now ready to communicate using the encrypted HTTPS channel for their traffic.

What really happens is illustrated in Figure 7.4. Alice's request goes to Eve's machine. Eve then forwards it on to the server, which uses its own private certificate C1 to create a reply. Eve's machine intercepts this, strips out the server's signature and uses her own private certificate C2 to create a new reply to Alice. Alice receives this and communications are achieved. All traffic from Alice to Eve is encrypted, and all traffic from Eve to the server is encrypted. But Eve now has the ability to decrypt all traffic in either direction, and read information such as passwords.

There is a weakness to this strategy. Eve can construct a certificate C2 that purports to identify the server 10.2.1.43, but it is not likely that she can get it signed by a trusted third party. For example, a company like VeriSign[W] or GeoTrust[X] might have some questions as to why you want a certificate identifying you as, say, PayPal. When Alice connects, her browser will try to warn her, as shown in Figure 7.5.

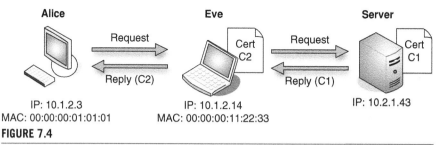

FIGURE 7.4

Eavesdropping Achieved

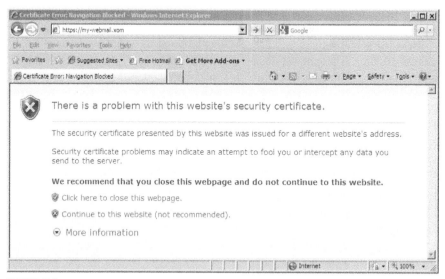

FIGURE 7.5

You Were Warned

[W]See https://www.verisign.com/index.html.
[X]See http://www.geotrust.com/.

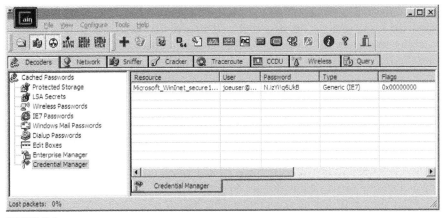

FIGURE 7.6

Password Capture with Cain & Abel

The message "intercept any data you send" is a strong hint as to what is happening. Of course, there are many sites out there with "self-signed" certificates, meaning they use certificates that are not signed by a trusted third party. People may be quick to assume that all is well, and just click the **continue to this website** link. After all, what's the alternative? *Not* checking your bank balance? You need to know! And after all, isn't your bank's security *their* job?

If implementing ARP poisoning sounds very hard to you, take heart. Conversely, if you think it is too hard to worry about it—well, many password sniffers, including Cain & Abel, implement ARP poison routing in a convenient manner.[Y] For Cain & Abel, this comes down to making sure that the tool is set up correctly and then clicking a single button to enable ARP poisoning. In Figure 7.6, Cain & Abel has been used to capture the password "N.izYi!q6UkB" – a very strong password – from an Internet Explorer 7 session.

DANGERS OF PASSWORD REPLAY

Password capture and replay poses a very serious threat to network security, and can be very difficult to guard against because it requires that people choose good passwords, keep track of them in a secure manner, do not fall prey to social engineering schemes, and are vigilant when using secure communications.

One immediate danger is that capturing a password on an otherwise innocuous site such as a personal Web mail provider could lead to compromise of other accounts because of password reuse. For example, corporate policy might require

[Y]And dsniff does, too. See the arpspoof tool that is part of the dsniff package. Likewise, Ettercap supports ARP poisoning, as do many other tools.

strong passwords changed relatively frequently. It is unlikely that Rob's Web mail password is the same as his password to the payroll system because he's required to change the latter. However, his VPN might use a certificate secured by the same password he uses for his Web mail. This might allow an attacker to get into his secure corporate e-mail, and from there an attacker might be able to get Rob's payroll password reset. If IT trusts sending passwords in encrypted e-mails that do not pass outside the secure corporate network, this strategy might work.

Replay attacks have dangers of their own because, as with software exploits, you may not know about them as soon as the bad guys do. Worse, if the protocol is itself weak, it may be days, months, or even (as illustrated by the NTLM case described earlier) years before the vulnerability is fixed. Critical infrastructure may depend on the protocol, so just disabling it is not an option.

Many protocols depend on cryptographic hashes for security. As time goes by, these hashes (SHA1, MD5, and so on) are studied and eventually may be cracked. Again, replacing the cryptographic hash at the core of a secure protocol is a nontrivial matter.

DEFENDING AGAINST PASSWORD REPLAY

Several proven technologies exist to avoid password capture and password replay attacks, but one of the most basic ways to resist password theft is to avoid the use of a single, static authentication token whenever possible. Although this is not always possible, it does provide the best means of security.

One method is for the user and the authentication system to augment a shared, static secret like a password with a dynamic, or changing, shared secret. The two must be properly combined in order to gain access. An example of this is the RSA SecurID.[Z] This uses a tamper-resistant device containing a clock synchronized to the server's clock. A shared key is used to generate a sequence of numbers; without the key, the number sequence is nearly impossible to predict from just a few observations. Each number is displayed and is valid for a period of time, and then a new number is generated. When a user wants to log in, they enter a fixed static secret like a password, and combine this with the current number displayed by the SecurID. Someone capturing packets would not be able to replay the authentication later on because the number used would no longer be valid. Even if the attacker got either the user's password or the SecurID device, they would still need the other piece of information to be able to gain entry. Although this is an excellent approach, it can also fall prey to the man-in-the-middle attack. The credentials cannot be permanently compromised, but the secure session can be hijacked using a technique like ARP poisoning.

Another authentication technique is to use one-time passwords. In this case, at login the server generates a challenge. The user looks up the challenge, say on a printed card, and enters the correct response. Each challenge/response pair is good

---

[Z]See http://www.rsa.com/.

for exactly one login. This is a very strong system, and can be combined with a static password so that loss of the card containing the challenge/response pairs would not compromise the system. Again, this can fall prey to a man-in-the-middle attack that hijacks an existing session. A one-time password system that is common on UNIX and Linux systems and is completely software-based is the S/KEY system.[AA]

One reason ARP poisoning attacks work is because layer two of the network does not have any built-in security. Fortunately, there are both software and hardware solutions to this problem. ArpON[BB] is open-source software for detecting and *blocking* ARP poisoning and spoofing attacks, and it runs on Linux and UNIX, including Mac OS X. Antidote[CC] is another open-source ARP poisoning detection system. Several hardware vendors, including Cisco,[DD] have implemented a technique called Dynamic Host Configuration Protocol (DHCP)[EE] "snooping" to detect ARP poisoning or spoofing. Finally, Arpwatch[FF] attacks the problem by watching for ARP messages that reassign an IP address, and generating notifications if this happens.

ArpON can operate in two different ways to defeat ARP poisoning: *static* and *dynamic*. Static ARP inspection works by assuming the ARP cache at program start is valid, and then defending it against modification. This works well if your network consists of machines assigned with static IP addresses. Dynamic ARP inspection works by first clearing the ARP cache, and then carefully monitoring any attempts to modify it and applying rules to prevent ARP poisoning. This works well if your network consists of machines assigned with dynamic IP addresses (DHCP).

THE FUTURE OF PASSWORD REPLAY

In 2004 then Microsoft Chairman Bill Gates, in his keynote address to the RSA Security Conference, predicted the end of traditional passwords.

> *"There is no doubt that over time, people are going to rely less and less on passwords. People use the same password on different systems, they write them down and they just don't meet the challenge for anything you really want to secure."*[1]

A few years have passed, and we're all still using traditional passwords. Bill was right; they are fundamentally flawed as a security measure. It also seems they are not going away any time soon.

There are just too many places you need to authenticate on the Internet. Some means is required; whether it is a password, pass phrase, or combination of questions

---

[AA]The S/KEY One-Time Password System is described in RFC 1760. A free implementation for the Mac is available from http://www.orange-carb.org/SkeyCalc/.

[BB]See http://arpon.sourceforge.net/.

[CC]See http://antidote.sourceforge.net/.

[DD]See http://www.cisco.com/.

[EE]DHCP provides a means to dynamically reserve an IP address for a host, based on the host's MAC address.

[FF]See http://ee.lbl.gov/.

and answers. Your Web designers and your users are all familiar with passwords, and you can't issue special hardware to everyone who registers on your Web site.

Without careful design, protocols are susceptible to replay attacks. Even in cases where protocols *are* designed to be resistant to replay attacks, a weakness in the protocol (as with WEP) can render the protocol susceptible. Finally, even if the authentication portion of the protocol is resistant to replay attacks, it may still be the case that a "man in the middle" can hijack a session and use replay *within* the authenticated session.

Replay attacks are, in some ways, analogous to buffer overflow attacks. They can be eliminated by careful design, and one must keep this in mind when designing an authentication system or protocol. The analogy breaks down, however, when we consider systems with deployed weaknesses. Eliminating a buffer overflow exploit requires shipping a patch. The patch can be tested, and installed on a machine-by-machine basis. For replay vulnerabilities, often the protocol must be *redesigned*. This makes it tough to eliminate the vulnerability, as both endpoints of any potential communication session must be upgraded to compatible, resistant protocols. It may not even be possible to upgrade some legacy systems, as software is no longer being developed for them. Many network endpoints are embedded devices, and the manufacturer may delay in releasing an update, or never release an update at all.

The problem of legacy protocols is often "solved" by allowing one endpoint to downgrade to the old protocol. This is obviously a serious vulnerability. You might have updated your servers to support the newest resistant protocols, but still they have to support older versions of protocols (such as NTLM and SSH-1) because of legacy hardware and software.

Because protocols that are susceptible to replay attacks continue to be designed and deployed, and because weaknesses continue to be discovered in the cryptographic systems that are used to protect against replay attacks, it is clear that replay attacks will remain a very deadly network attack for the foreseeable future.

SUMMARY

After reading this chapter, you should have a better appreciation for the security risks of password capture and password replay. Password capture and replay is a significant, ongoing threat to the security of networks. Because traditional passwords and protocols that are susceptible to replay attacks are not going to go away any time soon, this represents a significant security risk. Further, designing protocols to resist replay attacks requires careful engineering and analysis...so we can assume that even new protocols may be susceptible to replay attacks. Once a vulnerability has been discovered in a protocol, it can be a long time before a fix is available.

Fortunately, there are technologies to help secure against these attacks. The use of one-time passwords, hard-to-guess sequence numbers, and tools like SecurID can block the usual methods of password capture and replay. Sadly, these can still fall prey to man-in-the-middle attacks, made ever easier by well-designed and maintained automated tools. The fundamental message is to evaluate how and when users can authenticate, to establish reasonable policies, and to implement network security auditing. ARP poisoning can be detected on the network using readily available tools. Even so we can expect this network attack to remain deadly for a long time to come.

Endnote

1. See Kotadia M. Gates Predicts Death of the Password, CNET News, February 25th, 2004. Available online at http://news.cnet.com/2100-1029_3-5164733.html; (accessed 2/28/2010).

Index

If you've enjoyed reading about these attacks you will love *Seven Deadliest Wireless Technologies Attacks*, another book from our Seven Deadliest Attacks Series.

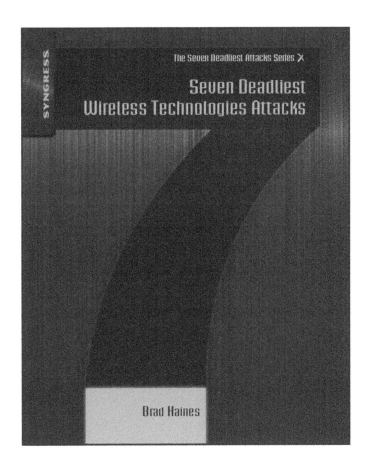

Radio Frequency Identification Attacks

INFORMATION IN THIS CHAPTER

- RFID Basics
- RFID Risks
- Physical Access Control
- RFID Meets Crypto

Radio Frequency Identification (RFID) is a technology that everyone hears about but most people do not fully understand. Its name is thrown about in terms of efficiency and modernization of commerce, and at the same time, it is associated with Big Brother and privacy invasion. In terms of security, it is a technology that is only starting to come into maturity for security, but it is so often misunderstood and the risks so underestimated that security is often completely forgotten.

Most modern office buildings have done away with physical keys in favor of proximity card systems. We've all seen them, the cards on lanyards being waved in front of the readers at doors like some magical "open sesame" command for the modern age.

At the DEFCON 17 hacker conference, it is widely known that a fair number of attendees are federal agents, some under their own names and some undercover, but all there to learn. There was quite a stir among many of them this year: those who thought they may have had their proximity cards cloned. A project, undertaken by Adam Laurie (major malfunction) and Zac Franken to raise awareness about RFID vulnerabilities, gathered more data than expected.

Their project consisted of a 125-kHz RFID reader and a large antenna hooked to a laptop. The laptop also had a webcam attached to it. All of this was in plain sight on a table in the conference area. Anyone walking up to the table with a compatible RFID card on their person would have it scanned and their picture taken with the webcam. The idea was to then scrub the data and put it on the "wall of sheep," joining other attendees who used insecure protocols to login on the conference network.

It turned out that their project worked better than expected and may have captured the data from the door access cards of several federal agents. For conference organizers, this was stepping into a gray area (more than the usual for DEFCON) that they thought best not to encourage, and during the "Meet the Fed" panel, it was explained to the assembled feds on stage and the audience what had happened and the implications of this. At which point Adam Laurie destroyed the memory card with the data without having given it more than a cursory glance. Afterward, many were heard to say, "We never thought of that."

RFID BASICS

RFID encompasses many technologies under one acronym. Pretty much, any technology that is used to identify something via a radio signal fits under the RFID umbrella. As most people know it, RFID is a short-range wireless identification system typically used for building access, for barcode replacements, and in identity documents and payment cards. Chances are that you have one or more RFID-enabled devices on you at any given time. Most people, however, have little idea how these devices actually work, which like most technologies, leads to security risks and vulnerabilities.

RFID devices commonly have two parts: the transponder and the reader/interrogator. When the reader queries the tag, it replies with some identifier, most basically an identification number (there can be more complex responses which are discussed later), which is received by the reader and some action is performed with that identifier. This may seem overly general, but there is no end as to what can be done with a tag and reader. The tag can be placed just about anywhere, and the reader can pass the identifier to a back-end system, which can cause just about anything to happen, from an account being debited to opening a window or updating a map. The RFID identifier should just be treated as input into a larger system.

RFID Systems

Most common RFID systems fall into two categories: active and passive. This usually denotes the power system involved with the tag, as well as how it behaves when not being interrogated. RFID at its heart contains a very small processor that performs some action when powered; however, the method of power does limit some uses.

Active Tags

An active device typically has a battery or some other power system. The device is always "on" and typically has a longer range than passive tags. These devices are broadcasting their signal all the time and can be received by any appropriate reader in the vicinity. Major examples of this are the ubiquitous EZpass in New York State and other U.S. states in the Northeast and other toll collection devices around the world.

Usually, active tags are larger due to their requirements for internal power. There is no end of the sizes and shapes available, but they are typically much larger than passive tags. The advantage of an active tag is the increased range due to the extra power. This is one of the features that make them very attractive for toll collection since cars do not need to slow down or get unnecessarily close to the reader – the toll can be collected automatically, almost without slowing down from highway speeds. This reduces the manpower required for toll collection, as well as decreasing bottlenecks and traffic delays caused by manual toll collection. It also means that travelers do not have to worry about insufficient change since the tag is linked to an account that is billed later via credit card or invoice.

There is a third type of tag, the battery-assisted passive (BAP) tag. These tags require an external signal to "wake up" but once they are, they utilize a battery to vastly increase their range. These can be classified as active tags due to the use of a battery, but for some uses, it may be useful to consider them separately. For the purposes of this chapter, they will be considered in the active tag category.

Passive Tags

Passive devices are the other side of the technology. These devices are unpowered until brought into proximity of the reader. The reader powers up the tag through a process called induction. A radio signal of a specific frequency is emitted by the reader to the tag. The tag's antenna is tuned so that the readers' signal induces an electrical current in the antenna, supplying electricity to a small capacitor. When the capacitor is at full charge, it powers up the chip on the tag, which then performs its functions, sending out its reply through the same antenna to the reader. This process repeats as long as the reader is in range and is energizing the tag. Being that there is no requirement for an external power source like a battery, these tags can be extremely small. Some designs are just slightly larger than a grain of rice; others are thin enough to be made into flexible adhesive labels and attached to just about anything. Some packaging options can be embedded in clothing, namely the sewn in tag.[A] There are many packaging options available, with the tag itself only taking a very small amount of space in the package. Figure 4.1 shows a variety of tags and a small hobby reader.

Since passive tags are powered up by the reader, this requires that the reader be much closer to the tag than in an active system. The signal powering the tag from the reader decreases in power with distance (the attenuation is proportional to the inverse square of the distance from the tag), so to increase the read range, one needs to increase the power to the reader. However, the tag only has a limited range on its capability to send signals back to the reader, so if the reader is too far away, it may be able to power the tag, but not able to hear it. This distance is usually a few inches to a few feet depending on the specific technologies and readers used. This is not a problem for a door access card or a credit card system, but is not optimal for a car traveling at 50 mph.

[A]In many jurisdictions it is mandated that RFID tags in clothing be removable, so they are usually found as attachments to the cloth tags already in the clothing.

FIGURE 4.1

A Variety of RFID Tags and a Small Hobby Reader

Passive tags are by far the most common type of tag and are used in payment systems (credit cards), in authentication systems, such as door access cards, in counterfeit detection, such as tickets to the Beijing Olympics and passports, and on products of all shapes and sizes for inventory control.

RFID RISKS

RFID is often talked about as either a security panacea or a nightmare. It all depends on which side of the risk you stand.

As a panacea, its main benefits revolve around the capability for electronics to stand up to attacks by counterfeiters and other nefarious persons. They also provide much more potential of an audit trail and granular control in a variety of ways for things like inventory tracking and building access.

As a nightmare, they stand out because society in general has a tendency to trust technology. If someone can successfully counterfeit or clone an RFID device, it is assumed that it must be legitimate, and often there is no further check beyond the existence of a valid-looking tag.

The benefits of the technology are also its weakness. Since it has the power to transform any industry it is used in, it has the effect of people believing it to be infallible and as such, not preparing for its possible failure.

An issue that always seems to come up with regard to RFID systems and security is their expected longevity of use. A business investing in a system probably expects to use that system for 10 years or more and often it does. Should a vulnerability or unforeseen risk emerge in that time, they would most likely have to replace most, if not all of the system – something that costs a great deal and they are unlikely to do.

Another issue is complacency: the system has been operating for 10 years and those in charge of it may not be aware that there has been a new discovery that destroys all their previous conclusions about the system. It was a secure system when they installed it and still is as far as they know. Related to this is cost-breeding complacency, a business not wanting to opt for a higher-security system because they don't feel at risk (yet!) and can save money opting for the cheaper and less secure system.

In the security world, things can change, literally overnight. A once secure system can resemble Swiss cheese with one piece of information. With the speed of information dissemination around the Internet, potential attackers can learn of these issues in minutes. To correct an issue in the software world, this typically involves a patch or simply upgrading the software package to a new version or a reconfiguration. In a system where the vulnerabilities are built into hardware, this becomes an infinitely more complex problem to solve. RFID solutions are definitely in the latter category of a hardware problem.

In order to alleviate a vulnerability, all readers would have to be upgraded (via software if possible, but possibly the hardware too) and every card would have to be replaced. In an installation where there are hundreds of readers and thousands or millions of RFID-enabled card or devices, this is a huge task that will take significant amounts of time and money.

PHYSICAL ACCESS CONTROL

In today's world, it is a necessity that certain groups of people need to get into an area and other people need to be kept out of the same area. This has been an issue since the first humans built a wall to keep someone out of their space. If you were a prehistoric cave man and you wanted to keep creatures out of your cave (and hopefully from eating you), you built a wall of some sort so they could not gain access. This caused a problem, however. If critters could not get in, that likely meant that neither could you, and you may well become something's lunch without the protection of your cave. So shortly after the first wall was built, something resembling the first door was invented. This can be thought of as the first access control. The early human knew about the door and how to move it to gain access to the cave, but the critters did not. If you were a human, you could enter. This is physical access control; one person or group can pass through some physical barriers but another cannot. Over the years, this evolved into bigger walls, drawbridges, moats, guards, secret handshakes, and eventually to early locks and keys.

In more modern times, this grew into several different methods, all with advantages and drawbacks. Modern keys and locks can be fairly secure; however, granularity of access is difficult and may require users to carry multiple keys, which can be lost, requiring locks to be changed at great expense to prevent the lost key from working if it fell into the wrong hands. Mechanical locks also wear and break, requiring specialized maintenance, and in general, require a fair amount of overhead to keep the system secure in a large facility.

Guards are a common method of access control, even today. There are some major disadvantages to guards, though. They are expensive, they make mistakes, they can be bribed, fall asleep, or become an insider threat themselves. Guards also are not very keen on keeping audit logs of every employee's movements throughout a facility. That said, a human guard has some advantages and can greatly compliment a technological solution as will be discussed in a bit.

In 1960, magnetic stripe cards were designed by International Business Machines (IBM) and used as access controls by the Central Intelligence Agency (CIA). Mag stripe cards (like credit cards) have their identifier number encoded on a magnetic strip that is swiped through a reader connected to a computer backend. These systems are still in use today but suffer from problems of worn out cards and worn out readers. As well, since the read head for the mag stripe needs to be accessible and needs to be fairly precise, exterior access was problematic with dirt, rain, and other elements fouling the mechanisms. These systems, though, laid the groundwork for today's modern systems.

Finally it has evolved to what most modern office buildings are equipped with, RFID proximity cards (so named because the card and reader activate when in proximity).

EPIC FAIL

In 2006, the United States began issuing passports with RFID tags implanted in them as a security measure. The tags, when a proper key was provided, would respond with a digital copy of all the information on the photo page of the passport. The idea was to make it harder for counterfeiters since they now had to alter the physical passport, and the contents of the RFID tag to match the person presenting it.

When the plan was announced, privacy and security advocates were not pleased. Public comments were taken in and as a result, some changes were made to alleviate some fears, namely of the possibility of the passport being read at any time, not just at the border.

The solution consisted of a layer of metal foil in the cover of the passport acting as a shield against the tag sending or receiving any RF energy. This solution, on a technical level, works. When the passport is closed, communication with the tag is not possible. However, the solution is self-defeating. Due to the thickness and rigid nature of the foil and how it is embedded between the layers of the cover, the passport naturally wants to "pop" open about 1 inch, rather than stay closed like earlier generations. This gap is enough to allow the tag to be read, thus defeating the point of the foil in the cover. A passport in a purse or in a loose pocket will naturally want to open, potentially revealing data. This has lead to the common site at border control of wrapping an elastic band around the passport to keep it closed or using a special shielded case with a clasp for the passport.

This is a fairly common sight at most modern offices with employees simply waving cards in front of the readers that grant them access. You can usually see a small plastic box beside the door with one or more LEDs on it, though not always.

These systems can work via active or passive tags. Most of the older systems have a thicker active card, about the thickness of two credit cards that contains a coil antenna, the RFID circuitry, and one or more coin cell batteries. Other systems operate on passive tags, powered by the reader, and are often the same thickness as a credit card. There is no standard package for a proximity card system; however, the "card" format is most popular and is often integrated with the employee's ID badge as well.

Proximity Cards

The use of an RFID proximity system has many advantages over previous methods. Since it is a contactless system (wireless), the card and the reader can both be sealed against the elements. This allows for exterior readers to put up with rain and dirt and not be damaged. It also means that neither the card nor the reader can ever really "wear out" through repeated uses.

The most common and most basic use is through a simple numeric identifier. A card is presented to the reader and is queried. The card transmits its identification number, and the reader sends this to the back-end system. If the numeric identifier is allowed to enter that door, it sends back an approval message to the reader, which then opens the latch or door. If the presented numeric identifier is not allowed, nothing happens and the door stays shut. All of this takes place in a matter of moments and the user just has to wave their card in front of the reader to start the process.

Proximity-card-based systems offer many enhancements to security over earlier traditional systems like guards and keys. The biggest of these is the use of unique identifiers. In a traditional key-based system, everyone with a key to a door had the same key. Short of a secondary method to verification, there was no way to tell which key opened the door. This caused issues since everyone with a key could point at everyone else and say they were the one who opened the lock. There was no way to leave an audit trail of who opened what and when with keys. With a proximity card system, each employee's card has a unique identifier, which is tied to their name in the back-end system. This allows for discreet logging of a specific employee accesses and provides auditing, in case there are issues later.

The use of unique identifiers also allows for a high degree of granularity of control over what a proximity card can have access to. Traditional keys posed the problem, that to have really granular control over access, separate keys had to be issued for each lock and properly distributed. This was a real headache to manage and keep organized and led to people often having more access than necessary since it was easier that way. A proximity card system allows for very granular control and can allow you to specify down to individual doors, if you so desired.

If an employee is terminated, it is a very simple step to disable all his/her access at once rather than trying to change locks or reclaim keys that may or may not have been copied. If an employee loses a card, it is also easy to simply deactivate the old one and issue a new one and apply the same rights as the old one. A lost key in the mechanical lock system meant that locks would have to be repinned and new keys made and distributed.

Depending on the system, the cards can activate more than just doors. Machinery, cabinets, dispensers, vending machines, and even computer logins can be integrated with the system to allow a single card to perform many different functions.

Physical Access Control Failures

For a moment, it's worth looking at the concept of authentication since that is what this system is all about and where its failures lie. All the system is doing is taking the unique identifier and granting or denying access based on that identifier. This is where the problems creep in – it is just granting or denying based on the identifier. There is no mechanism to verify who is presenting the identifier.

There is an old saying within security referring to authentication: "Something you have, something you know, something you are."[B] This describes the different general methods a person has to authenticate to any security system, technological or not.

"Something you have" is simply a physical token that you must possess to gain access. The most common example is a ticket to a concert. You only need to have the ticket to get in: they don't care who is holding the ticket, just that you have it. The computer equivalent would be a hardware token like a smart card or a security certificate.

"Something you know" is simply a secret that only an authorized user would know. Most people know this as a password. From the login password to your computer to a kid's clubhouse or secret handshake to identify membership in a club, it does not matter who it is, as long as they know the password, handshake, dance, or whatever is being used to authenticate.

"Something you are" refers to biometrics. While this can be as complex as fingerprints, or retinal scan, it can be as simple as your friend, the club bouncer, recognizing your face and letting you in. Some unique element of you as a person is being used to authenticate into the system.

Generally within the security field, any system should integrate at least two of these things. "Something you have" and "something you know" could be a smart

> **NOTE**
>
> A special note should be made that while a traditional key is definitely "something you have", if more than one user has the same key, there is little point in using it as a security token. The logic of "Something you have" and of all parts of the authentication triangle is that every identifier is unique and thus can be traced back to a specific user, ensuring nonrepudiation. A common key among users means that now only one factor (a password, or biometric) is all that is left to authenticate.

[B]This is a security principal often taught as part of basic security classes. An example use is http://cs.cornell.edu/Courses/CS513/2005FA/NNLauthPeople.html

card and a password. "Something you are" and "something you know" could be a fingerprint scan along with a password. Any system should be built with at least two of these things (optimally, all three) required to authenticate to the system. This better prevents an attack on the system.

The corollary to the above saying is "Something I lost, something I forgot, something I was."[C] This emphasizes the failings of each of the individual authentication methods given above and highlights why they should be used in concert.

"Something I lost" is fairly obvious. If a user is issued a physical device to authenticate, he or she can lose it. Losing a key is the most obvious form of this that we've all dealt with. In the case of a proximity card system, a card can be lost or it could be stolen. As an attacker obtaining the card grants, you access simply by possessing the card, same as if you beat up someone in the concert parking lot and took their ticket.

"Something I forgot" should be very obvious to anyone who has ever worked technical support. Users will forget things. Passwords, handshakes – all can be forgotten and grind access to a halt. The subtext of this is that passwords can be divulged, sometimes innocently shared, written on a sticky note, or just guessed. Other times, they can be "discovered" through coercion, blackmail, extortion, or torture. Again, if you know the password and that is the only authentication method, then there is nothing stopping you once you know the password.

"Something I was" is something many people don't think about as much. This concept is a bit more of a gray area than the others. If your authentication method involves a biometric, it is hard to lose or forget your fingerprint or retina, but it also comes with new considerations. What about injury? If a fingerprint biometric is used, what if someone injures that finger or loses a whole hand? Are other fingers or biometrics enrolled? From an attacker's perspective, this one is harder since it requires physical access to the person they are trying to authenticate as. You might try to coerce the user to authenticate for you. You may try to forge or copy the biometric such as lifting a fingerprint and making a fake hand. It may also mean the more drastic step of amputation of a hand or finger to bypass a fingerprint system.

WARNING

An attacker removing a digit to authenticate as someone has happened. In Malaysia, in 2005, an accountant was car-jacked for his Mercedes S-class car. The car was outfitted with a fingerprint lockout device, enabling only the owner to start the car. After carrying around the owner in the trunk for a while to restart the car when needed, the thieves became frustrated and relieved the owner of part of his finger before dumping him on the side of the road (http://news.bbc.co.uk/2/hi/asia-pacific/4396831.stm). In any system, a determined attacker will find a way to bypass or defeat a security system, up to and apparently including amputation.

[C]As seen on a Shmoo group sticker at Shmoocon 2005 and mentioned among security circles ad nauseam.

The idea is that the difficulty and an attacker's level of commitment to the attack increase with each additional method. A password can be guessed remotely, but a password with a hardware token is much harder. Now an attacker has to physically interact with the victim, something most common attackers have no interest in. Using all three means that the attacker must have the password, the hardware token, and the biometric all present to authenticate, a fairly daunting proposition for all but the most dedicated attacker.

TIP

Some biometric systems use voice prints to identify a user. A person's voice can change over time, be affected by a cold, even by their mood, or by what they had for lunch. As such, to avoid high failure rates, these systems often have their tolerances tuned down, sometimes to the point where a recording of the user's voice will suffice to authenticate with the system. For obvious reasons, in high-security situations, this may be undesirable.

Any biometric system selected should take into consideration the failure rates and issues associated with a system and their suitability to the expected application.

Proximity cards' main failure is that they are usually a single factor form of authentication, namely the unique identification number. This means that, barring any other methods, an attacker just has to present the unique identifier to the reader to gain access. There is nothing that ties the unique identifier to the person it was issued to and whose access we are impersonating. There is also nothing in this type of system that ties the identifier to the proximity card it is expected to be on.

Cloning RFID

Since RFID proximity cards are wireless based, this gives an attacker an advantage over something like a physical key. Unlike a physical key that you would need to physically remove from the victim to copy,[D] the wireless nature of the proximity cards means that they can be read at a distance and do not need to be removed.

A large number of proximity card systems in use today, particularly older installations, only use a simple numeric identifier to authenticate. There is no encryption or any verification done on the card, other than to check the number received against a back-end system. This also means that there is no authentication by the card of the reader that is interrogating it. It will respond to any compatible reader and present its numeric identifier to it. This is very useful for an attacker since they can simply wave a reader past a pocket or purse of their victim and the card hands off the identifier. The attacker can then take this information and write his or her own copy of the card to use as they see fit.

In 2003, an engineer by the name of Johnathan Westhues took to tinkering with proximity cards and understanding how they work. Through his efforts, he was able

---

[D]While there are methods for duplicating keys from photos at a distance, this still requires the victim to remove the key from his or her pocket or purse to view it, limiting the time an attacker can obtain a picture. A wireless interface is available all the time for attack and just requires physical proximity.

to reverse engineer the protocol of the Motorola flexpass and understand what was being transmitted by the card and how it interacted with the reader. He continued his efforts and began to build a card simulator in order to interact with readers and understand how the cards worked. After a while and after some revisions, he built his own combination reader and card simulator, since both share many of the same parts. The device, called the proxmark, is not much larger than a credit card and only twice as thick and is dead simple to operate. It consists of two buttons, one for "reader mode" and one for "card mode." "Reader mode" turns the unit into a 125-kHz RFID tag reader that you can hold by any compatible tag and it will read its unique identifier and store it in memory. The "card mode" button simply replays the stored tag information. This means that he could walk up to someone and surreptitiously scan the contents of their proximity card, walk over to the secure door and replay their card, whereupon he would be granted access as if he had presented the real card.

Over the next several years, he has revised his device and greatly improved its capabilities. As of February 2009, the Proxmark 3 is the latest revision and supports most 125-kHz and 13.56-MHz tags (the two most common frequencies) and can read and emulate most any ID-only tag out there.

> **NOTE**
>
> All of the schematics, bills of materials, and designs for the Proxmark are available on Johnathan's Web site at http://cq.cx, if you want to build one yourself. If you are not inclined to build one yourself, completed devices are for sale at http://proxmark3.com/. A warning though that in most jurisdictions, cloning a card that you are not otherwise already authorized to have is probably illegal. You should only experiment on systems and cards you own or have express permission to experiment on.

The existence and availability of this device now means that an attacker can now clone many common proximity cards and simply replay them to gain access. There is still the issue of how to get to where we need to go in a building. If we are after secret research or something as valuable, its access is likely to be restricted to a few specific employees. This means that we cannot simply clone just anyone's card, we need to be sure to get one that will get us access to the area we need to in order to do our dastardly deed.

Role-based systems that allow granular access to certain areas seem like a decent way to limit employee access. They can only have access to where they need to be and can even limit access to certain times. However, an attacker can often use this to his/her advantage.

Optimally, these roles would be rigid. Only people with a real need to access a certain area would be granted access, and it would be strictly enforced. However, most businesses are a bit more political and pragmatic than that. Typically, those with legitimate access will have no limits on their access hours in case they work late, assistant staff may need to get access to do things on behalf of their bosses.

In a perfect world, Owner/CEO/Head honchos of the business have no real reason to go into some areas: their employees report things to them, and they don't need to actually go there themselves. People in these positions, however, tend to not like the idea of being locked out of anything or any limits put on them, and as such, their access is usually unrestricted and covers most, if not all, of areas and times.

As an attacker, we can use this by targeting the bosses and cloning their identifier. It can be as simple as sharing an elevator or in line for coffee. Sometimes, this does pose a problem though since the bosses of some organizations are not easy to access. There is one person, however, who will tend to have complete or nearly complete access to a facility: the janitorial staff. Just about any office has a cleaning staff who take out the trash, wash floors, and so on, typically at night; these people need to have their own access to enter areas to clean them. As an attacker, it's probably a lot easier to bribe or steal a janitor's identifier than the CEO's. One could walk up to a janitor as he is coming on duty and shaking his hand, and thank him for a good job, while your other hand silently clones the contents of the proximity card. Later that night, you can return and move about the building freely by simply replaying the janitor's card.

In either scenario, the audit logs (if any) will show the victim of the cloning as the one moving about the building. At worst (as an attacker), this will show the path you moved through the building. At best, it will direct the blame for your activities to the victim and away from you.

Minimizing the Risk

While it is possible to clone ID-only chips, that is by no means the complete end to using them for physical access control, but it did mean that it was not reliable as a stand-alone system. Many things can be improved in order to increase security of these systems.

One of the first methods to improve security is to actually audit the logs. Often, logs are ignored until something happens and then they are cursed for not being complete enough. Taking the time to evaluate if everything is being captured that you would need in a crisis will go a long way. In addition, automated auditing and alerts of the logs can be very useful in spotting inconsistencies and potential problems. If the enforcement of access controls is tight enough (scanning on both entrance and exit of a door), you can monitor for unusual activity such as Bob entering the building twice, or Bob's card being used at opposite ends of the building when there's no way he could have traveled that far. You can also look for situations where people are deviating from their normal schedules. A secretary should generally not be in the building at 3 A.M. Automated monitoring of the logs and alerts can help stop something before it starts.

In addition to auditing the logs, audit the enrolled cards. Periodically verify that only current employees are in the system and that access is as it should be. Employees who leave the organization should have their access immediately disabled but in case that does not always happen, periodic audits will help catch those situations. Also audit for test cards, often a new system will have one or several test cards issued with full access for the installers and administrators to test the system and make sure that readers work, doors open, and so on. Often, these identifications are not removed from the roles since the cards are destroyed. If the identifiers issued are sequential, it may be possible for an attacker to count backwards and generate cards from a known low access card to try and find some of the first issued cards.

As much as there are issues with security guards, they have one advantage in that they can think. If they are properly trained, they can add a formidable layer of security. Typically, a guard at an employee entrance will get to know the people coming in every morning. As an attacker, this is a real problem since we likely look nothing like the person whose card we spoofed. Some systems allow a human guard to see the logs of who is authenticating at the door and perhaps even an employee photo and may be able to spot the inconsistency of our access and detain us. This does require that guards not become complacent and be distracted watching TV or surfing the Internet, but it is a definite hurdle to overcome. Guards, however, are expensive and often their role is that of visible deterrent, rather than an active participant in the authentication solution. However, their presence can allow for more security than a completely technical solution alone.

Other ways to improve our fictitious scenario is to issue shielding sleeves for employees' proximity cards. These metallic sleeves block the signals from readers and prevent the readers from powering the tags, thus minimizing the risk from surreptitious cloning if employees actually use them. Actually explaining to employees the risks and implications of having their cards cloned can help get them on your side and prevent them from exposing the cards unnecessarily. Explain to staff that wearing cards on a clip or lanyard away from the office exposes them to unnecessary risk. Removing them and even placing them in a pocket will make them less of an obvious target. Other simple things like not leaving their cards in glove boxes where they can be easily stolen is common sense that occasionally needs to be reenforced by security and IT staff.

Even after all that, the risk still remains that cards can be cloned and that access is fairly easy to obtain. Often, these systems will be installed and in place for years and even decades. It's pretty certain to say that early designers and adopters never thought that their systems would ever still be in use when attackers gained the sophistication to attack them reliably. If the threat posed is great enough, upgrading or replacement of the system is about your only option.

RFID MEETS CRYPTO

One of the more obvious solutions for RFID as authentication is the introduction of cryptography into the process. The tag and the reader both have to prove a shared secret to one another before they will grant access. Cryptography has been used for decades in the computer world for authentication with great success. So why is it that it was not there in the first place?

RFID chips are small – very, very small. They vary depending on the make and model, but sometimes the actual silicon chip is smaller than the head of a pin. There is also very little processing power available on these chips. They are that way partially to make them easy to produce; it makes them cheap, and it also means their whole package will be small, which increases their applications.

With the diminutive size, it is a challenge to cram solid, known trusted algorithms. In the first few generations of tags, this just was not feasible. So manufacturers and designers did what they had to do in order to provide for the market demand for secure chips and broke a general security understanding, it's not a good idea to make your own crypto.

The most recent example of these types of system is the MIFARE Classic (http://nxp.com/#/pip/pip=[pfp=53422]|pp=[t=pfp,i=53422]). The MIFARE Classic system is a 13.56-MHz tag built by NXP Semiconductor. The low cost and availability at the time made it ideal for a great many applications, the significant of which were physical access control and fare systems for public transit. NXP boasts over 1 billion cards in circulation, accounting for about 70% of the market worldwide.[1] This, along with its usage as a fare system in London (Oyster card) and the Boston Subway (Charlie card) made it a very interesting target for research.

To secure communications, the MIFARE Classic uses a challenge-response authentication system. The challenge-response system is like a conversation you would have with a bouncer at a door to a club. You want to tell them the secret password number "5" to get in, but if you say it out loud, it could be overheard and anyone could get in. So you establish a mathematical system to prove that both of you knows the key without saying it out loud. This system must be hard for someone to reverse the process to get the number themselves. To keep it simple, the algorithm will be to take the secret number and the random number, multiply them together, and square the result.

You walk up to the bouncer and he picks a random number and says "My challenge number is 6." He has already calculated the expected result using the secret number 5. You calculate (in your head): $6 \times 5 = 30$, $30^2 = 900$. You reply to the challenge: "900" and issue your own challenge to see if he is actually the bouncer: "My challenge is 2." You already know that the answer is $2 \times 5 = 10$, $10^2 = 100$. If the bouncer replies with 100, you have both proven you know the secret and can proceed. If his response to you is wrong, you can walk away not trusting him or at the least, wondering about his math skills. If your response to him is wrong, he can throw you to the curb and move on to the next person in line. Fortunately for RFID, the results are less dramatic for failure. This is obviously an over simplified example as the encryption algorithms are (usually) much more complex, but the process is similar.

The MIFARE Classic system uses a challenge-response system to authenticate the reader to the card and the card to the reader without divulging the secret key over the air. The reader sends out a request for the unique identifier. The card replies with a 32-bit random number, the challenge. The reader takes this random number and computes it with the secret key both the reader and card share and the resulting 8-byte response is sent back to the card along with a 32-bit random number. The card finally replies with a 4-byte response to the reader and the unique identifier is now sent to the reader in an encrypted form. The card knows that the reader's response to the challenge should match with what it calculated and the same applies for the reader. This way both devices have authenticated to each other and the system can open the door.

The weakness was that the encryption system, called CRYPTO1, was built by NXP to fit on the chips in the tag and was proprietary. NXP made sure to keep the algorithm secret so that no one could understand exactly what was occurring. In the above example with our bouncer, it is necessary to keep our algorithm secret since someone who knows it and overhears the response can simply reverse the process and figure out what the key must be (square root of 900 = 30, 30/6 = 5) and then respond appropriately to any future challenge and gain access. This is a classic case of security by obscurity.

Originally launched in 1995,[1] the system quickly showed up everywhere and continues to be used today. It was not until 2007 that researchers were able to get anywhere in cracking the system. At the 24C3 conference in Berlin in December 2007,[2] Henryk Plotz and Karsten Nohl announced that they had successfully reverse engineered the CRYPTO1 encryption algorithm.

Their method was very labor intensive but ultimately successful. They took the integrated circuit (IC) from the tag, which measures approximately 1 millimeter by 1 millimeter, and very carefully scraped off the outer layers of the chip, exposing the transistors within. Then, with the help of a microscope, they photographed the chip in very high detail. This process was made even more complex by the fact that these chips are multilayered and they had to scrape off each layer individually, each only a few microns thick. After they photographed all the layers, they set about identifying the area responsible for encryption through some detective work. Once they had the proper section of the chip isolated, they used some image recognition software to identify the function of each transistor and how it interacted with others. After all this, they were able to reconstruct the internal logic at work within the chip that handled the encryption and reconstruct the algorithm. This breakthrough meant that they now understood the internals of the encryption and they could begin looking for potential vulnerabilities.

One of the interesting vulnerabilities they discovered was that the pseudorandom number generator (PRNG) in readers was stateless. Stateless meant that it did not keep track of its previous state between power cycles. These allowed them to power down and power up the reader and use the same pseudorandom number for multiple attempts, a big help in the encryption analysis world. It also showed that the random number generator on the tags was 16 bits, which means that it was a very small pool of random numbers and they were likely to repeat.

The reverse engineering of the algorithm was a huge step in being able to clone a card. Since compatible cards are easily available (anyone can buy them), it was just the matter of determining the key used on a legitimate card and transferring that to another card.

A few months after the presentation by Plotz and Nohl, in March 2008, a team from the Digital Security Group of the Radboud University Nijmegen in the Netherlands was able to recreate the algorithm themselves and began a cryptanalysis of the CRYPTO1 algorithm. It did not take them long to find several critical problems that led to the system being well broken. Their Youtube video caused a minor stir in the security world (http://www.youtube.com/watch?v=NW3RGbQTLhE)

One method involved attacking the reader. Using a modified proxmark3 board, they attempt 4096 authentications with the reader and record the results. Those results are fed into a 1-terabyte lookup file that contains all of the possible states of the algorithm, which also correspond to the keys. The attacker can simply generate this file in an afternoon and use it for any MIFARE Classic system they encounter. The results of the queries to the reader are looked up, which reveals the key.

Another and even simpler method of recovering the key involves no lookup table at all – it simply uses a weakness in the algorithm to give the attacker the state of part of the algorithm at the end of the transaction (even though it failed) and, with a little computing power, this is enough to determine the key for the system.

Once a key is recovered, the attacker can now use a mobile reader configured with the key to surreptitiously interact with a users' card, and since they authenticate properly, they can read all the information on the card. Once they have that information, they can write it onto another card and it will behave exactly as the cloned user. The Netherlands team demonstrated this with their Youtube video demonstration. In it, the attacker walks up with a laptop to the reader and using the proxmark3, collects a number of authentications and then returns to his accomplices who then use that data to recover the key. They then use the proxmark3 again (this time configured with the key) to wirelessly sniff the contents of a users' card. They then take that information and write it to a whole stack of cards. Each of those cards now authenticates as the cloned user.

NOTE

The cryptanalysis and internals of the attack could be a book in and of itself and is glossed over here. The original paper describing these attacks is available at http://www.sos.cs.ru.nl/applications/rfid/2008-esorics.pdf

---

Considering the number of cards deployed and that many secure facilities use this technology, some people were none too happy about this revelation. NXP was certainly not happy. The team planned to present their findings at the Esorics 2008 conference in Istanbul, only to be challenged in court by NXP who filed an injunction to prevent them from presenting their research. The courts eventually found in favor of the researchers and allowed the presentation to proceed.

EPIC FAIL

This scenario was later brought to the forefront again at the DEFCON 16 conference in 2008. Several students from Massachusetts Institute of Technology (MIT) were scheduled to deliver a talk about the Boston area subway system and several vulnerabilities they have found throughout, from physical to network, social engineering, and ticketing. The Massachusetts Bay Transit Authority (MBTA) took exception to the guerilla research done to their RFID payment card, named the Charlie card. The students had basically implemented the attack by the Netherlands group and had applied the attack to the MBTA readers. The MBTA filed a last-minute federal lawsuit against the students barring them from delivering the presentation. The Electronic Frontier Foundation (EFF) stepped in and was able to get the lawsuit dismissed, but only after the conference was over, which is what the MBTA seemed to want in the first place.

The students' slides were posted to the Internet by the MIT student newspaper at http://tech.mit.edu/V128/N30/subway/Defcon_Presentation.pdf. The court documents are available online through the EFF at http://www.eff.org/cases/mbta-v-anderson

SUMMARY

RFID is a tricky technology to secure. It is wireless, and as such, communications can be read at a distance and captured. Due to their small size, the options for encryption are limited and often rolled by the manufacturer themselves instead of peer-reviewed algorithms, which can lead to them being defeated with ease.

In the end, any system based on RFID should ask the following questions from the beginning: "What do we do if this fails?" "If a tag is cloned, what will the effect be?" "Is there another layer of protection that will minimize the impact if this occurs?" "What is the organizational structure around the use?" "Is it possible to audit its use and monitor for irregularities?" All are tough questions that must be answered.

RFID is a young technology, and developers and society are still adapting to what it all means. There is no simple solution and it is up to the integrator/user of the system to actively think about what the system's authentication scheme means in a grand sense. Simple authentication with a card may be good at limiting access to the front door of a building from the general public, but perhaps not the crown jewels. RFID-enabled credit cards may seem convenient, but one must weigh the convenience of this against the possibility of a drive by skimming of the credit card details. In that particular case (1 factor), physically swiping the card and requiring a signature is a better (2 factor) and more secure solution to keeping your credit card safe.

Endnotes

1. www.nxp.com/#/pip/pip=[pfp=41863]|pp=[t=pfp,i=41863]
2. http://events.ccc.de/congress/2007/Fahrplan/events/2378.en.html

Printed and bound by CPI Group (UK) Ltd, Croydon, CR0 4YY

03/10/2024

01040342-0010